PRAISE FOR *BUSINESS DEVELOPMENT BEGINS HERE*

"At last there's an author who is able to make a very clear distinction between 'sales' and 'business development' instead of hovering somewhere between the two. With that difference clearly articulated, Tom Watkin's new book casts a bright spotlight on the critical steps needed to build individual, team, and organizational business development capability through his carefully crafted *triple A framework*. Whether you are just starting out in business development, need to refresh your own personalised approach, or have recently assumed responsibility for an organization's BD function, *Business Development Begins Here* is an essential starting point."

—Emeritus Professor Gary Martin FAIM FACE, Chief Executive Officer of the Australian Institute of Management Western Australia

"This is a must-read for anyone involved in B2B biz dev! In a very manageable 184 pages, Tom Watkin crystallizes the key components of both strategy and tactics for assessing opportunities, targeting well-qualified prospects, and taking prompt action to close business. While very useful as a 'kick start' for first-time sales/biz dev professionals, it also provides a powerful but easily digestible framework for running a company's business development efforts."

—Ed Zier, Former Chief Operating Officer of Baseline Financial Services in New York City, and Author of *Undaunted: Leadership Amid Growth and Adversity*

"In a world full of complexity and ambiguity, it is a rarity to come across a book that is pragmatic, refreshingly straightforward, and easy to read and understand. Tom Watkin draws on a wealth of his own experience and that from others in related fields supported by simple illustrations to bring the book—and business development—to life. His triple A process offers a step-by-step guide to the confusing world of business development. It is a must-read for anyone starting out in business development, and a timely reminder and revision for those already in it!"

—Simon Hollington, Co-Author of *Post-Pandemic Leadership: Exploring Solutions to a Crisis*

"Tom's passion for business development shines through in the book. Like he states in the book, you must have a passion for what you sell, and there is no doubt where Tom's lies. This is why the book is such a great inspiring read, full of relevant information and illustrations for those just starting in business development and for the seasoned professional. I found myself constantly nodding and thinking, *What a great idea and what a great way to frame* it—and now my notebook has so many new ideas to grow our business. Thanks, Tom. I am definitely getting a copy of this book for all my team."

—Wayne McFerran, General Manager of Western Australia and Northern Territory for Tetra Tech Coffey

"*Business Development Begins Here* by Tom Watkin is the guide I wish I had when I started out in business development. Tom incorporates many resources, has complete examples of applying the knowledge of the *triple A framework* he has developed, and leaves you with plenty more resources to further your growth. What's more, it's easy to read and to follow. This is a must-have book for anyone who is a consultant or in a business development role."

—Howard H. Prager, Leadership Consultant, Executive Coach, and Author of *Make Someone's Day*

"Filled with practical thought, approach, and process, Tom Watkin's book, *Business Development Begins Here,* taps into the real difference between sales—the transaction and business development—and the relationship and process.

"Tom makes a compelling case that the growth-driven business developer (GDBD) begins with a mind shift from order taker to order maker. From there, it's as simple as following his *triple A framework* methodology: Assess. Aim. Action. I especially found it helpful to have visuals that reinforced his concepts and a list of additional reference sources at the end of each section.

"Regardless of where you are in your business development journey, you will find this book to be a simple, step-by-step guide to grow your business."

—Dr. Troy Hall, Talent Retention Expert, Author of the Bestselling Titles *Cohesion Culture: Proven Principles to Retain Your Top Talent*, and *Fanny Rules: A Mother's Leadership Lessons that Never Grow Old*

"This book is a comprehensive, end-to-end how-to on business development to help your business achieve strong revenue growth. Tom has distilled his personal experiences into a simple, three-step process that is full of practical insights and lots of useful tools and information all with one focus in mind: business growth through an efficient and effective systematized business-development framework.

"What I like most about the book is that you could read it front to back or dip in and out of it, as needed. The action summary at the end of each stage, along with the top tips at the end of each chapter, are very useful. This is a book that can set you up for ongoing business success."

—Shirley Anne Fortina, Director and Principal of the POD Consultancy

"Podcasts were not relevant to the advice I was looking for. Websites were not engaging for me. However, Tom's book is built for the consulting world. It helped me analyze the competition, identify opportunities that weren't clear to me, and derive a forward plan for scaling growth. After working through the book, I am no longer 'waiting by the phone' but am instead being proactive and finding the confidence to contact clients now that there is a strategy with direction."

—Alyce Sala Tenna, Team Leader of GHD

"Business development is a complex and ever-changing field. Tom Watkin's book is a much-needed guide that makes it accessible to anyone looking to improve their business.

"Unsurprisingly, a practical approach to increasing sales requires considerable planning, strategy, and the capacity to draw on various resources and platforms. Tom Watkin's *triple A framework*—assess, aim, and action—is a road map for success that is easy to follow and provides actionable steps for achieving purposeful revenue growth.

"The author's clear writing style makes complex topics easy to understand, and his examples and references bring concepts to life. This book is for you if you are looking for a practical guide to help you transition to business development or upskill your current process."

—Juana-Catalina Rodriguez, Keynote Speaker, Advisor,
Award-Winning Author of *Unsettled Disruption*

"In the world of business development there's a lot of noise out there. Things that sound good in principle that everyone's heard of but lack substance to it. Then there's this book. It incorporates a well thought through cross section of everything that makes up business development, written in a deep yet highly relatable way. The structure makes it so easy to take action immediately after reading. Tom is a clear expert in his field which can be seen in the clarity of his framework and most importantly connection around purposeful work."

—Chris Smoje. Customer Service Expert of chrissmoje.com

"A practical, real, and relatable sales experience. Tom has clearly applied his years of experience and education, which he is not only passionate about but also willing to tell the world. This is a story I will most certainly share with my team of up-and-coming sales professionals."

—Simon Martin, Business Line Manager of Epiroc

"Starting in environmental engineering consulting some twenty years ago and being promoted into a business development role, I wish I had a resource like Tom Watkin's *Business Development Begins Here.*

"Tom breaks business development into an easy-to-use system comprising three stages—assess, aim, and action. I could relate to his accounts of real live examples used to explain the stages. The book supports the foundations for someone entering a BD role but also acts as a refresher of the fundamentals of a well-versed business development practitioner."

—Martin Brownlee, Environment Manager

"More than a book on his own experiences, Tom has provided practical and clear frameworks fit for newcomers, experienced professionals, or established business owners alike. The book encourages you to apply these frameworks to suit your situation and, most importantly, take systematic action. *Business Development Begins Here* will provide an easy-to-implement resource for those with business development as a part of a new role, a graduate at the beginning of their career, or a business working for their market share."

—Sam Mueller, Managing Director and Owner, West Soil and Water.

"Simply brilliant! Practical, pragmatic and resourceful. A must read for early-stage ventures and budding entrepreneurs."

—Sharad Bhat, Co-Founder of an Early-Stage Start-Up

"There are so many books on sales. Tom finally introduces businesses to the world of true business development. His *triple A framework* of assess, aim, and action is a winner. He captures brilliant research from Michael Porter, Ansoff, and other contemporary authors to produce an easy-to-read business development one-stop guidebook. If you are entering the business development world, it's a must-read."

—Ray Middleton, Vice President of Business Development
at a Fortune 50 Corporation

Business Development Begins Here: Your Practical Guide to Achieving Purposeful, Repeatable Revenue Growth

by Tom Watkin

ISBN 978-1-64663-784-3

Published by

◤ köehlerbooks™

3705 Shore Drive
Virginia Beach, VA 23455
800-435-4811
www.koehlerbooks.com

BUSINESS DEVELOPMENT BEGINS HERE

Your Practical Guide to Achieving
Purposeful, Repeatable Revenue Growth

TOM WATKIN

VIRGINIA BEACH
CAPE CHARLES

Dedicated to those professionals struggling to make the leap into business development. I hope this book simplifies the topic for you, bringing confidence and success.

TABLE OF CONTENTS

INTRODUCTION

Welcome to the world of business development. A realm of revenue, opportunity, and customer relationships. To be successful, a business developer has to juggle a lot of balls in the air and must draw upon a wide variety of skills. Moving into this role, you now have the responsibility of funneling revenue into your organization, either through fee-paying work or the sale of products and services.

There is an expectation that you will be talking to customers, pursuing leads, and writing proposals, often while maintaining the other aspects of your job. Success requires careful strategy, planning, and the ability to draw on a range of tools and platforms. Systematic communications are necessary, not only with potential customers but with the teams inside your organization. Most of all, as a successful business development professional, your actions need to be purposeful. By this I mean that your actions must be focused on bringing in sales that further the overall intent of your organization.

When I was younger, I joined an international engineering consultancy with a focus on the technical delivery of water projects. Within a few months, I was lucky enough to be promoted to the team leader role. This comprised a strong business development component, alongside efficient leadership and project delivery skills.

In my new role, I had to keep the projects rolling in and the team busy. To be honest, I didn't know where to begin. Sure, I had a few industry contacts from previous roles, but I wondered how I could progress from there.

Luckily for me, Jim, our team's experienced principal, was keen to guide me in the right direction. Together, we planned and tackled business development inside and outside the company. Jim showed me the power of networking within the organization, which was vital because our team often supported the outcomes of large projects won by other departments.

For a few weeks, colleagues in other business units showed surprise that we could offer our capability in-house. Building those internal relationships through networking and undertaking some soft marketing within our own business made a noticeable impact to our funnel of projects. Jim and I also developed a rudimentary sales plan for communication with our customer base that kept us regularly talking to the right customers.

Jim's guidance was invaluable. It laid the foundations for what business development entailed and started me on a journey of learning what I would eventually codify into this book.

Not everyone is so lucky to have a mentor on hand to guide them toward the right path. At the time of writing this book, I had not been able to find any formal courses that teach the basic fundamentals of business development. Instead, I found a plethora of short video courses available on an array of different topics, with nothing tying them together into a useful consolidated system. It seems to me that this forces an individual business developer to have to pick their own topics and weave them together to work out their own approach. This observation has been reinforced by my conversations with many new business developers in the consulting world, who often felt they had been left to work it out on their own.

I have written this book to act as a guide for those thrust into a business development role for the first time. My aim is to get you thinking about the market you play in, the stakeholders you should consult, and the customers you need to pursue. I want to guide you, step by step, to achieve strong revenue and growth-focused outcomes.

HOW TO USE THIS BOOK

'␣ve written this book as a manual for newcomers transitioning from technical specialization to business development. With this end in mind, I've presented a systematic framework that sets the foundations of business development. This framework should be adapted to the needs of the user. However, I recognize that readers picking up this book will be at different stages of their business development journey. As such, everyone will be using the content differently. I've divided the readership into three broad user categories:

New—readers who have little to no experience with the business development discipline. This may include consultants gaining seniority, startup entrepreneurs, or small business owners with an eye on systematic growth.

Upskill—professionals with some experience in business development who are looking to improve their skills. This group could contain senior consultants whose business development efforts are falling flat or a business owner looking to install a manageable sales process.

Immediate Action—those who find themselves thrust into a business development role with little to no preparation time. These might comprise leaders parachuted into failing business units, those making snap promotions, or those with positions where immediate changes to revenue are critical to success.

Each group will use this book differently. I provide guidance on which sections are most relevant below.

Alternatively, feel free to use this book as a manual and dip in and out of the topics of interest. If your business development process needs work, check out the "Systematic Sales Path" section. Perhaps you want to understand your market better, then follow the methodology presented in the "Mysteries of Market Mapping." View it as a toolkit to help refine and improve different aspects of your business development proficiency.

There is a "Top Tips" section at the end of each chapter. This provides a snapshot of the key points and details some further reading to expand on the themes. Check these out before diving into each chapter to help you pick which sections to focus on.

New to Business Development

Some readers have been promoted into a role that includes business development but have no training in the discipline. Often, you're grounded in a technical discipline, which is extremely beneficial, allowing you to talk to your customers from a place of authority.

I advise reading this book in order, from start to finish. Learn the basic principles before working through the *assess, aim,* and *action* stages of the *triple A framework*. Make notes on the exercises as you read. Get an understanding of the company vision, map your market, and define your customers.

Each stage of the book builds on the last. By the time you finish, you will have a defensible assessment of your market and company capabilities, three plans informing the direction of your business development effort, as well as a growing series of systematic processes and actions to keep you disciplined and focused on increasing your revenue.

Upskill Your Business Development

For someone who already has experience with business development, there is an opportunity to cherry-pick the parts of the *triple A* system that benefit you. As a start, I would recommend looking at the following sections:

- The Mysteries of Market Mapping
- Who are Your Customers?
- In-House Relationships

These areas offer clarity on your market and target customers. They will also guide you through developing relationships within your own business. This will help ensure you are aiming your business development effort in the right direction.

Developing a *tactical action plan* would be the next point of call—making sure that you have a robust plan or tool that is systemizing and prioritizing the necessary action. Feel free to use your existing tool or app, but make sure it is of practical use.

Reading the "Action" chapter is probably going to be most useful. The "Systematic Sales Path" provides simple yet effective processes to incorporate consistency into your way of work. This will help in qualifying leads and only pursuing opportunities that will add value to your business.

Use this chapter to revisit the way you contact your customers and see if there are opportunities to be more systematic in your approach. The same is true of your proposals and quotes—can these be produced with more consistency and efficiency?

Finally, the last part of the "Action" chapter involves the adaptive feedback of market intelligence to the rest of the business. Refining the way you channel the market and customer information back into the business can have a huge impact on how it adapts to change. It can also alter the perception of your value as a business developer.

Use the sections listed above to refine your current way of doing things. Use the content to interrogate your present approach and adjust for improvement as required.

Immediate Action Business Development

For someone who enters a role where business development activity is required immediately, a different approach to this book may be needed. First, I would suggest negotiating some time with the leadership to allow for a proper assessment of the situation. If this is not possible, here are a few suggested actions to help you hit the ground running.

Undertake the following activities as a priority, while commencing a work-through of the *triple A framework* in parallel. The adaptive feedback loop is crucial here. Information gleaned from customer discussions and feedback must link back and inform the planning and direction of the implementation. The priority actions include:

Develop the profile of your ideal customer. Discuss with your team what the attributes of your ideal customer look like and develop a profile around this. You can check this as more data is collated during future customer and stakeholder discussions. This will give you a good indication of which customers to pursue first.

Create a customer matrix. Use the *ideal customer profile* to develop a *customer matrix*. Include your top current customers and a handful of priority targets, all with a burning need for your company offering. Use the matrix to determine your initial customer priorities.

Develop a preliminary *tactical action plan*. Using the customer priorities above, identify key personnel within each priority customer, and feed them into your *tactical action plan*, making sure to assign due dates to each.

Meet existing customers to ask for feedback on past performance. Make this an immediate priority to get honest feedback on why they buy from you, what works, and what doesn't. Make sure to loop this information back into the work being conducted on the *assess* stage and to the relevant internal stakeholders in the business.

Implement the *systematic sales path*. Keep your actions aligned to the process detailed in the "Systematic Sales Path" section. Discipline around this now will make things much easier as you progress. Keep the *tactical action plan* updated and live.

Adapt and refine the *tactical action plan*. As you work through the *triple A framework* (in parallel with the immediate actions), keep the findings and output from the framework feeding into and adjusting the *tactical action plan*.

While the above actions let you hit the ground running, make sure to spend time on the *assess* and *aim* stages to keep up with long-term direction and focus.

THE BASICS

Unfortunately, not every business has a dedicated sales function. Perhaps they perceive themselves to be too small or, as is often the case, the senior operatives or leaders are expected to do the work through their ongoing client relationships.

The importance of maintaining a strong focus on business development is often overlooked, and we regularly hear people say that their product or service is so good that it should sell itself. How can the product sell itself if the customer does not know about it?

The business development function is key to forging the link between the activities of the organization and the wider marketplace. In doing so, they form an integral part of the adaptive organization, pushing feedback into and out of the company, allowing it to adjust pricing, products, and services accordingly.

Good business development practice enables you to grow your company with purpose—by pursuing opportunities that align with your company vision. You must assess the market niche that you play in, define your preferred customers, and then move to pursuit through action. Systematic and planned customer communication keeps your product or service in the forefront of your customer's mind.

Often when staff with technical skills rise through the ranks, particularly in the consulting space, business development responsibility begins to enter their role description. What do you do when you've been promoted away from your area of expertise to a role that now encompasses quite a different skillset? How can you transition from someone focused on doing the technical work to someone who brings in the work?

This guide is intended to act as a playbook, providing a step-by-step system that will allow you to undertake thoughtful and intentional business development—ultimately enabling you to grow the business and keep yourself and your team fed.

First, we need to understand the basics. What is business development, the sales ecosystem and the sales funnel? How do they interrelate? Understanding these concepts lays a foundation for the implementation of the systematic framework later in the book.

Business Development: A Simple Definition

First, we need to define what business development actually means. Unfortunately, there does not seem to be one universally accepted definition. Business development is often seen as another word for sales. In my opinion, this is doing us a massive disservice.

True enough, business development is, at its core, about the sale of products or services. But this should be coupled with the long-term goal of developing and growing the business. Business development is more than just closing the deal. It requires strategic thinking and decision-making behind who to approach, how to approach, and the identification of new opportunities that align with the long-term success of the company.

In my opinion, the real difference is that sales can be considered short-term and transaction based—while business development is focused more on the long-term strategic outcomes of the business. Therefore, my simple definition of business development is: **the act of sustainably growing the business.**

The core components of any business development role should be:

- **Sales and Pursuit**—an aggressive pursuit of sales opportunities that align with the company's vision and intent.
- **Customer Relationships**—the development of robust, trust-based relationships with customers, allowing for honest two-way communication.
- **Commercial Integrity**—a strong commercial acumen with the ability to sell products and services at a profit margin that aligns with the company goals.
- **Productive Paranoia**—an avid following of quoting (leading indicator) and revenue (lagging indicator) numbers.
- **Market Intelligence**—a deep understanding of the market, the key players, and consequences of any changes therein.

- **Offering Intelligence**—a deep understanding of the problem that your company solves.
- **Adaptive Feedback Loop**—a conduit for information between the market and the company, to ensure that customer and market feedback is heard and acted upon.
- **Customer Service**—a polite and professional approach in all dealings. You are the face of your organization.

Business development should be considered a core function of every business. The business development leader should have a seat at the leadership table. There is no one better suited to align company decision-making to the point of view of the customer. These leaders operate in the heart of the marketplace, allowing them to identify shifts in customer behavior and initiate meaningful change to adapt accordingly.

Gwynne Shotwell, an accomplished aeronautical engineer, is a great example of a strong business development leader. She quickly transitioned into sales and business development (BD) while maintaining her engineering skillset. Shotwell saw a gap in Elon Musk's SpaceX venture and joined as employee number seven, as the vice president of business development. Using both her technical and BD abilities to successfully position the space explorer as the industry leader made her an invaluable part of the company—so much so that she was promoted to president and chief operating officer (Vance, 2016). The argument for having business development integrated into the company leadership could not be stronger.

The Interconnected Sales Ecosystem

A *sales ecosystem* is much like a natural ecosystem in that all the components are interlinked and changes to one will impact the others. Navigating this ecosystem is a key part of the business development professional's role. Figure 1 shows a simplified diagram of the sales ecosystem's components and those interactions that are important to this role.

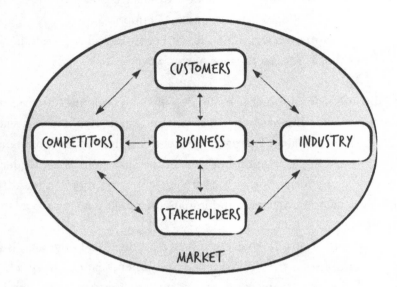

Figure 1: Sales Ecosystem

A summary of the key components follows:

- **Business**—the organization that produces the product or service that the business developer represents. This can be thought of as the organism surviving and growing within the ecosystem.
- **Industry**—the wider industry or industries that the company and customers operate within. Examples could be mining, financial services, healthcare, real estate, civils, and construction, etc.
- **Market**—the area in which the industry operates, usually signified by geography but can be broader. This can be considered the larger environment and may contain multiple industries.

- **Customers**—companies and individuals with a need to purchase the product/service. These could be existing or prospective in nature. The revenue from the customers is the sustenance that the company needs to survive.
- **Competitors**—competitors are those companies and organizations that are competing for customer revenue.
- **Stakeholders**—other organizations and individuals that play within the industry and market. These can take the form of strategic partners, suppliers, influencers, consultants, and government regulators. This group can be thought of as the web of other organisms competing for space and resources within the ecosystem.

Is Your Sales Funnel Full?

An organism can only survive if it is fed regularly, and a business is no different. It requires a steady input of cash to maintain its viability. It is the role of the business developer to navigate the sales ecosystem and use it to keep a steady stream of opportunities, leads, quotes, and sales flowing into the company. The traditional way to visualize this is the *sales funnel*.

Figure 2: Simple Sales Funnel

Fundamentally, the funnel comprises the stages of effort required to get a sale. Imagine this as a water funnel—your marketing leads (digital advertising, face-to-face meetings, and social media activity) are poured into the top. Some of these leads are genuinely interested in your company and become opportunities for a sale. A few of these opportunities will develop into sales, bringing much needed revenue through the door. A simple sales funnel model is presented in figure 2.

A basic sales funnel process comprises the following stages:

Leads—leads take a couple of forms. Firstly, these are people/ businesses who have shown enough of an interest in your offering to reach out to you. Secondly, they are projects or tenders that strongly align with your company offering. A full funnel of leads is generally gained from customer relationships, marketing efforts, and an understanding of what is happening within your market.

Lead Assessment/Qualification—to thoroughly pursue each lead can be a large waste of time and resources. Each lead must be quickly assessed and qualified as worthy of further pursuit. Don't waste time on leads that will not go anywhere.

Opportunity Pursuit—the qualified lead is now considered an opportunity, and time is taken to understand the customer involved, their drivers, and what problem they are looking to solve. Any gaps in understanding need to be identified.

Phone call—best practice is to call the key customer or stakeholder to learn more about the opportunity, establish or reinforce a trust-based relationship, and fill any gaps in the opportunity. The power of a phone call to the right person is significant and can really make the difference between winning and losing the opportunity.

Proposal—present your company offering to the customer. Your proposal should spell out the value of your offering and needs to comprise more than just a price.

Follow up—once the proposal has been received, give the customer some time to absorb the contents and follow up. Ask them if they need any clarifications or if they have any feedback. This can provide a chance to adjust the proposal to bring it in line with the customer's expectations. It also gives you an opportunity to gain insight into how the offering is perceived, allowing changes to be made to future proposals.

Sale—close the deal and secure the revenue. Now your team must deliver.

It is easy to see that if the leads at the top of the funnel reduce a little, the knock-on effect to the sales and revenue generation can be catastrophic. Keeping the funnel filled should be of prime importance to the business developer and to the business.

A good rule of thumb is that opportunities should value at least three times your monthly sales target. However, this may change depending on industry and organization.

We will expand on the sales funnel in later chapters, but it is important to understand the general process that must be followed to keep your business nourished.

The Makings of a Strong Business Developer

The role of a business development professional is more involved than most people appreciate. I've met and talked with many successful business developers over the years, and I've come to see that they share a number of common characteristics. I have distilled these into eight attributes that I believe are essential to becoming, what I call, a growth-driven business developer (GDBD). These attributes are summarized in figure 3 and explained in more detail below.

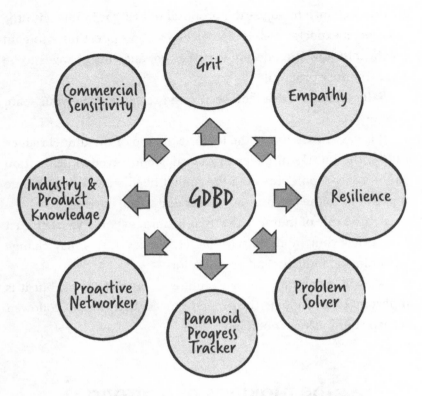

Figure 3: Components of a Growth-Driven Business Developer

Grit—a disciplined determination to succeed, use of the daily systematic tools provided in this book, and the willpower to maintain pursuit of priority customers and opportunities.

Empathy—the ability to commiserate with others and consider things from their perspective. A real understanding of the problems your customers and stakeholders face can help with your ability to frame your offering appropriately.

Resilience—in the never-ending attempt to gain new customers and opportunities, you must develop a thick skin and be able to accept rejection. Customers may not always have the time, or inclination, to meet or take your call. You can't let this get you down. Some customers are not yet ready for your offering. Make an action to loop back to them at a future date and move on to the next customer who *is* ready for your offering.

Industry and Product Knowledge—for customers to trust your solutions, you must have a comprehensive knowledge of your industry and the products or services that your company offers, as well as a good understanding of the niche in which your company offering sits. Becoming a specialist in that niche will have customers seeking you out for solutions.

Problem Solver—customers are looking to buy your product or service because they have a problem that needs solving. Looking for customer problems to solve and finding ways to overcome them is critical for company trust and credibility.

Commercial Sensitivity—a GDBD with no commercial sensitivity is a dangerous entity. An understanding of the underlying financial situation of your company offering is critical. How much profit is made per unit, and what are the ramifications of dropping the price? It is easy to achieve sales targets if you drop your fee lower than every other competitor. It is also easy to destroy a company if you sell your products or services at a price point where the company loses money.

Paranoid Progress Tracker—how can you know you are successful if you do not measure success? A GDBD must measure leading (opportunities) and lagging (revenue) indicators and be actively pushing to keep both above the line.

Proactive Networker—keeping your company offering in people's minds requires proactive networking across a variety of customer contacts and internal and external stakeholders. To really succeed, the networking needs to be systematic to prevent important contacts being missed. There is no requirement to be an extrovert, but you must be comfortable meeting people, engaging them with pertinent questions, and most importantly, listening.

Love Your Product

Having the attributes of a GDBD is one thing; however, you must also have a real belief in the product or service you are representing. There are salespeople who are overconfident enough to believe they can sell anything—regardless of their feelings toward the product. Those of us who have experience, and a conscience, know you cannot put your best into selling anything unless you believe in it. Donald Miller sums this up best in his book, *Business Made Simple*, when he writes, "Do you believe in the product you sell? Do you believe you can solve a customer's problem and change their life? If you don't, quit. I'm serious. Just walk away from the company and find a mission you believe in".

Having worked in the sales function of a company where I didn't believe in the product, I can tell you it can be extremely demoralizing. It takes an extraordinary level of energy to find the enthusiasm needed to be successful. It can also create a strong feeling of dissonance with the work you are doing and give a feeling of being insincere with your customers.

In my own case, I took Donald's advice. I spent some time exploring what I enjoyed about work and the types of services I was enthusiastic about. As it turned out, this was easy for me to define. The environmental sector was where I had knowledge, experience, and the ability to make a real impact with the work we were doing. When my energy was harnessed and focused on products and a mission that I could really get behind, customer discussions became a hundred times easier. I truly believed that our services added real value to the customer projects. As a result, winning opportunities became easier too. You must believe in what you are selling.

Be Proactive

I had a colleague a few years ago who was a real hero when it came to selling. He was proactive, did deep dives into his product offering, and had real enthusiasm when it came to solving his customer problems. I considered him a true GDBD.

I caught up with him shortly after he had joined a new company as a member of their sales team. Expecting him to be kicking goals left and right, I was surprised to hear that he was extremely disappointed with his new role. When I asked him what had gone wrong, he explained that the sales team of six people did nothing except sit by the phone waiting for it to ring.

There was no objective, no sales plan, and absolutely no systematic process for reaching customers. Each salesperson hoped that their phone would ring enough times for them to meet their targets that year. To add insult to injury, when my colleague tried to implement customer meetings, systematic sales calls, and market stakeholder discussions, he was met with derision from coworkers and leadership alike. Not long after we spoke, he told me he'd found another company that aligned more closely with the ethos of a GDBD, and he's resumed his goal kicking.

This story highlights the difference between an *order taker* and an *order maker*. An *order taker* sits at their desk, turns on their computer, and waits for the sales to roll in. They are purely reactive and at the whims of the customer. They live or die by what others do.

However, an *order maker* takes charge of their own destiny, understands their product, assesses their market, aims their focus in the right direction, and concentrates on systematic action to reach out into the market and bring the customer to them. They champion their product or service at every turn. Which would you rather be?

Introducing the Triple A Framework

To the uninitiated, the sales ecosystem and sales funnel can feel a little overwhelming. There are a lot of balls that need to be kept in the air at once. This is made much harder when business development forms only part of your role description, and other work commitments are competing for your time.

To help guide you through the practical workings of business development, I have formed the *triple A framework*. This has a cyclical structure that guides you through the process of business development (see figure 4). The framework is there to steer you toward strategic planning and systematic action to ultimately increase the revenue entering your business.

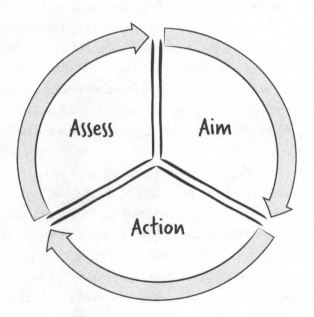

Figure 4: Triple A Framework

It can be summarized as follows:

- **Assess**—assess the strategic intent of your company, product offering, customers, and internal and external environments.
- **Aim** (Plan)—you must aim your business development action toward achieving the goals of your company. Understand the available marketing options and develop an aggressive strategic, operational, and tactical plan with a systematic cadence to maintain daily, weekly, and annual business development activity.
- **Action** (Execute)—execute systemic pursuit and opportunity development within the sales ecosystem to grow long-term revenue. Act as a conduit of information and feedback between the customer, market, and your organization.

Within the context of the framework, I will discuss the concept of five-minute marketing as a way of acquiring a variety of customer touch points with your customer base. These simple and cost-effective marketing tactics allow your target customers to become familiar with your brand, products, and services, feeding leads into the top of your sales funnel.

I have written each section of the framework to define and explain the key components of the process, before providing an example of that process in action. So, grab a pen and paper, and write down your ideas as you go. This will allow you to create the beginnings of a robust and practical business development plan that you can implement immediately.

THE BASICS—TOP TIPS

Business development is more than sales. It requires systematic, strategic planning and decision-making behind who to approach, how to approach, and the identification of new opportunities that align with the long-term success of your company.

—The business developer must navigate the sales ecosystem. This is an interconnected system comprising the business, market, industry, competitors, stakeholders, and customers.

—A Growth-Driven Business Developer (GDBD) should work on the following: grit, empathy, resilience, industry and product knowledge, problem-solving, commercial sensitivity, paranoid progress tracker, and proactive networker.

—Believe in the product or service that you sell. If you don't, it will create dissonance in the way you work. If necessary, move on to one you do.

—The *triple A framework* is designed to guide you through strategic planning and systematic action to keep your business development on point. It comprises the repeatable structure of *assess* (purpose, goals, and market), *aim* (planning), and *action* (systematic execution).

THE BASICS—FURTHER READING

I've made the recommendations below to get you thinking about business development in a wider context.

—Donald Miller does a good job of explaining how sales and marketing fit into the wider business in his book *Business Made Simple*.

—For a great take on how sales are perceived today, read Dan Pink's book *To Sell Is Human: The Surprising Truth About Persuading, Convincing, and Influencing Others.*

—*The Challenger Sale: Taking Control of the Customer Conversation* by Matthew Dixon and Brent Adamson gives a solid methodology for conducting customer conversations.

—*Blue Ocean Strategy* by Renée Mauborgne and W. Chan Kim is a great read to get you thinking about how to frame your company offering differently so it stands out on its own.

Business Example—Introduction

In an effort to bring the ideas within this book to life, I will be using examples to demonstrate how each section can be implemented in a business situation. Though fictional, I have based them on the real-life experiences of myself and several of my business development colleagues. I ask you to use your creativity here—imagine yourself to be a newly promoted consultant who is starting the journey from technical specialist to GDBD.

You are a contaminated land consultant for a global multidisciplinary engineering consultancy, Weyland Consulting Services (WCS), and have spent the last ten years running land investigations across your city and the surrounding region. Recognizing your technical abilities and strong performance, management has increased your responsibility through a well-earned promotion.

Now you are leading a team of three consultants, comprising two junior field operators and one very experienced principal consultant. The contaminated land discipline has been identified by leadership as a growth sector, and your remit is made very clear. Not only must you ensure that the team delivers on their projects, but you must lead the business development effort to grow the team within your city and the wider region.

While you understand the basic concepts of business development, you find yourself a little unsure where to start. Like any growth-focused professional, you reach out to your mentor who shows you the *triple A framework*. They are certain that this will help you begin the systematic implementation of your business development effort, in addition to the other leadership and project delivery priorities now on your plate.

As we progress through the three stages of the *triple A framework*, we will explore your journey with WCS, and learn how to implement the framework's structure.

TRIPLE A: ASSESS

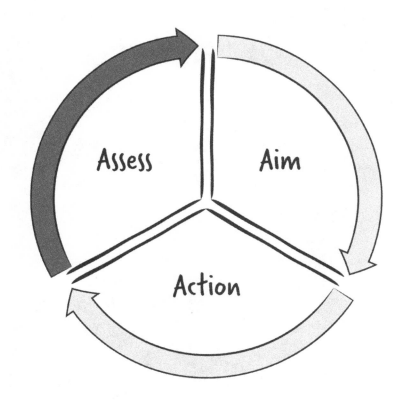

The *assess* stage of the framework requires you to appreciate the specifics of the sales ecosystem that you are operating within. To gain that understanding, define what the strategic intent of your organization is, how your product offering differentiates itself, and what defines your customers. A strong assessment of the sales ecosystem properly frames the planning (*aim*) and execution (*action*) stages that follow.

I must make clear that the *assess* stage does not comprise a super-detailed quantitative data analysis; rather it is a broad assessment that allows the shaping of a robust business development plan that is straightforward to execute. Many technical entrepreneurs fall into the trap of getting hyper detailed with their market analysis. They spend an inordinate amount of time and resources collecting and scrutinizing market and customer data for no significant gain.

It is better to have a broad assessment that can be shaped following feedback from customer and market interactions than to have a hyper detailed assessment with no customer interactions. I believe that the *assess* stage described below achieves the right balance between being data-driven, quick to achieve, and practical in application.

Defining the Strategy

The strategic intent of a company can be defined as its future intentions and direction. What does it want to become, and what does it intend to offer to the market? The long-term and short-term goals of the company will act as a compass for the business development activity.

Once appointed to business development responsibility, it is easy to become overawed by the scale of opportunity. This can lead to vigorous, high-energy activity but no focus on where that energy is directed. Often, this manifests in contacting potential customers only as they come to mind, with no clear tactic on how to get them to meet with you or understand your offering. A lot of effort will be wasted approaching customers who are not suitable while high-value targets may be missed.

You may develop a robust plan and start pursuing it relentlessly, but unknowingly, your effort may be spent on the wrong division, with no support from head office. Unfortunately, I have fallen into this trap. I was leading the Australian sales effort for a large European company. I could see that the mining industry in Australia was one of the biggest in the world and that we were not taking advantage of this massive opportunity. To my mind, there was a huge gap that could be filled by our product offering; running the numbers, the proposition was extremely compelling.

I armed myself with a plan, which detailed the target companies and the role titles of the people we would need to talk to. With high energy, I began the assault. But as I opened up meetings, it began to dawn on me that our initial offering was not compelling enough for the mining companies. They needed a slightly more niche offering. This niche aligned with some projects I knew were being run by our research and development team in Europe. I took my findings back to the bosses, explained where we were at, and looked for support for a trial, only to find that the senior management wasn't interested.

Their efforts were being placed into industries with more strategic value to the company, which resulted in no support for my plan, and a lot of wasted effort on my part. If I had interrogated the company's intentions and gained a better understanding of their longer-term goals, I would have realized that mining did not play a prominent role in their global strategy. Perhaps the hours and money I invested could have been put to better use elsewhere. My effort could have been channeled toward more strategically appropriate customers, with the mining opportunities only being pursued when time and resources were available.

The solution is to understand the purpose of your company and align your plan with it. That is not to say that outlier opportunities should be ignored, but you need to understand where the majority of the company resources will be funneled.

Before you start any business development activity, you need to determine the strategic intent of the organization, including its vision, purpose, and direction. Defining this purpose points you toward the end goal. It provides guidelines and boundaries to keep your business development activity aligned with the desired outcomes of the organization. The company-wide intent needs to be combined with the objectives of the business unit, division, or product line that you are representing. This will then inform the structure and direction of your business development activities.

Company Vision and Objective

In an ideal world, the company vision and objectives should be readily available and easily understood by all employees; however, this is often not the case. There may be pithy taglines and mission statements framed on the office walls, but the clarity around their actual meaning is often clouded. There are hundreds of words written about the need to clarify the company purpose and vision, which are far beyond the remit of this book. But a crucial part of business development planning requires that the vision and intent of the organization be clearly understood.

Develop clarity. Ideally, sit down with the leadership team and gain an understanding of what you need. At a minimum, the following questions should be answered:

- What is the purpose of our organization?
- What are the key aspirations of our organization?
- What makes us different from the competition?

- What market do we play in now?
- What markets do we want to play in for the future?
- What do we want to look like in three years?
- Where does our business development effort fit into the above?

Business Unit Vision and Objective

Once the strategic intent is understood at an organizational level, it is time to determine how this relates to the specific business division, product line, or team that you represent out in the marketplace. Again, if this is not clear, sit down with the team and work it out together. A few questions to consider include:

- How does the business unit work toward the organization's vision?
- What are the key aspirations of the team?
- What are the niche differentiators in-house and in the marketplace?
- What are the short-term and long-term objectives?
- What resources are available?

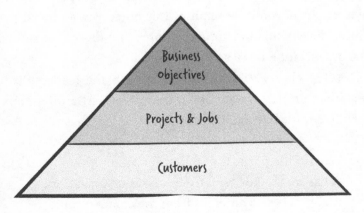

Figure 5: Planning Hierarchy

A useful way to look at this is to use the planning hierarchy presented in figure 5. Starting with the business objective in mind, the hierarchy establishes the projects and jobs that your company wants to undertake. This, in turn, determines the customers that must be pursued in order to win these projects and jobs.

The hierarchy allows a rudimentary road map to be drawn of the direction and growth of the business unit over time, forming an excellent compass that determines where the effort should be pointed.

Getting the answers to the five questions above and developing a resource planning hierarchy will provide clarity around the strategic intent at the organizational and divisional levels, and it will keep the business development effort aligned with the purpose and outcomes of the organization as a whole.

Target Expectations

The strategic intent of the organization will inform the targets and expectations against which the business developer will need to deliver. Typically, this will take the form of revenue achieved, but it may also be measured in terms of team utilization, profit, or another metric, particular to the organization at hand. Having the targets of the company, business unit, and team laid out clearly with measurable metrics sets the stage for future performance.

The business development function will also be assigned targets and *key performance indicators* (KPI). Compare these against the goals and intent of the company. Do they align, and will they be adding to the ultimate victory of the company? At the end of the day, the targets need to be commercially viable for them to add value. Revenue needs to bring profit into the company. An alignment check is needed to ensure that the future business development effort really does add to the bottom line of the company.

A sales team is often given revenue targets that they must meet to achieve bonuses for the year. Here is a brief scenario to show where targets can be misaligned with the company goal and cause major problems.

For example, the company GoBig Products assign aggressive revenue targets to their team, coupled with large bonuses if they are met. In an effort to win this bonus, the business development team get to work assigning large discounts to get big orders across the line—with no commercial checks in place. This leads to a situation where the team appears to be humming along, sales flying through the door, but production is barely keeping up.

Staff numbers are increased to compensate, adding more cost to the bottom line. The business development team is amassing huge bonuses aligned with the large revenues. Life is good.

But no one has checked the commercial viability. Each product is actually being sold at a significant loss. Before you know it, GoBig Products is losing money, files for bankruptcy, and jobs are lost. The moral of the story is a simple one—make sure the targets and expectations make sense.

What Is Your Unique Offering?

Every successful business is different. Each have their own diverse ingredients, which make up the "secret sauce" of how they do business. This goes beyond the individual characteristics of their service or product and involves unique processes, systems, and personnel within the organization. Look how these apply to the company as a whole and for the individual teams. These factors will shape the way you present your offering to the customer through conversations, marketing material, and proposal wordings.

Start with Why: How Great Leaders Inspire Everyone to Take

Action by Simon Sinek will get you thinking about the unique purpose and differentiators of your business and how to articulate them to staff and customers.

Some points to consider:

- What problem does your offering solve?
- How does your offering compare to your competitors?
- What is unique about your offering?
- What is unique about your team?

I ran an asbestos removal company for a while. Asbestos is a very emotive subject that can create a lot of unease. Our offering provided a professional service that completed the work with all the correct safety procedures and paperwork in place. The team wore clean uniforms and behaved professionally. Our strongest selling point was that we offered a professional service doing everything safely, greatly minimizing the risk to the current and future occupants and owners of the property.

Believe it or not, the lack of professionalism and care by the majority of our competitors meant that this was a huge differentiator within the local market. It highlights the point that your unique offering does not need to be complicated to be competitive.

A common complaint I hear from leaders across industries is that the sales or business development team often promise customers things that the service/technical/product teams just cannot deliver. This shows a misunderstanding of the company offering by the business development team and a lack of communication between the two departments.

Communication is the key to keeping your offering competitive. The business development team do not need to be technical experts, but they must have a strong relationship with the technical/delivery department to enable the teams to work through solutions together.

Take the time to understand your offering; gain enough knowledge to hold meaningful conversations with the client. This is easier when moving into a business development role that aligns with your previous technical background. However, entering a new industry or dealing with an unknown product offering requires time and a willingness to learn. Do not be afraid to ask for help. Talk to the technical team and learn from them.

Commercial Placement

Back in the early 1980s, Michael Porter published a book called *Competitive Strategy: Techniques for Analyzing Industries and Competitors*. One of his key models is the generic competitive strategies. Though coarse in its approach, this can be a good indicator of where your offering is being presented commercially. At its core, the model utilizes two characteristics to define your company offering:

- **Scope**—does your offering target a narrow or broad customer base?
- **Competitive Advantage**—is your offering advantage based on being the cheapest or on its unique differences?

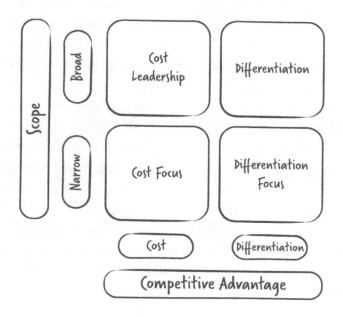

Figure 6: Porters Generic Strategy (2004)

The overall company scope and competitive advantage are plotted along the horizontal and vertical axes, allowing you to plot your company offering on the matrix and determine the generic strategy that it fits into (figure 6). These strategies are:

- **Cost Leadership**—no frills; winning on cost alone.
- **Differentiation**—creating uniquely desirable products and services to a broad market.
- **Focus**—offering a specialized service in a niche market.
- **Cost Focus**—offering a no-frills, cheap service to a niche market.

For example, consider a dams and tailings consultancy servicing the mining industry. They would plot within the differentiation focus quadrant as they offer a specialist service to a niche market. Meanwhile,

McDonalds, the fast-food giant, sits firmly within the cost leadership quadrant, offering low cost meal options to the mass consumer market.

While these strategies have coarse definitions, it allows the business developer to think broadly about how to approach their target customers and frame a message suited to their market. Approaching customers with a *cost leadership* mindset is very different to a *differentiation* mindset requiring widely contrasting conversations.

For example, I have seen environmental consultancies employ both models to great success, though the customers and opportunities pursued by each were largely different. A *cost leadership* environmental consultancy might focus on government contracts where low price is the governing factor. Alternatively, the *differentiation* consultancy would focus on larger industry where strong defensible scientific work is required for community engagement and licensing requirements. The latter can justify charging a higher price.

Prioritizing Products and Industries

Often, a business developer finds themselves responsible for a number of products, service lines, or industries, and it can be difficult to determine which to prioritize. A quick assessment can be made using the GE/McKinsey Matrix (*McKinsey Quarterly*, 2008). This methodology plots the company offerings or industries on two simple axes:

1. **Industry or Market Attractiveness**—commercial potential of the market or industry, i.e., potential to make money.
2. **Business Unit Strength**—ability and skill level of current staff to develop that industry or market with the offering being assessed.

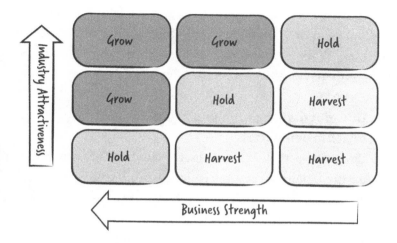

Figure 7: GE/McKinsey Matrix (2008)

The original form of this analysis is conducted with a high level of detail. However, for simplicity of use, I suggest splitting each axis into high, medium, or low. Once plotted on the matrix (figure 7), a general strategy for each offering can be determined. These strategies are described as:

1. **Grow**—strong business development effort and investment. Aggressively hunt for opportunities.
2. **Hold**—medium business development effort and investment; farming opportunities from existing customers.
3. **Harvest**—limited business development effort. Act on opportunities as they arise. Do not pursue.

The GE/McKinsey Matrix, coupled with Porters generic strategy, provides a fast assessment of where the product offering sits, the broad commercial strategy, and an indication of which product or service lines the business development effort should be focused on.

Another quick assessment tool that aids with prioritizing different products within a portfolio is the *product life cycle* (Levitt 1965). Plot the product and service offerings on the graph in figure 8 using annual sale volume and time the product has been in circulation. Each will fall within a different stage, each with their own broad strategy. A summary of each stage is presented below:

1. **Introduction**—new product. Hunt for new customers and establish brand trust.
2. **Growth**—established product. Pursue new customers and ensure quality service to retain existing customers.
3. **Maturity**—well established product. Farm existing customers; customer retention is a priority.
4. **Decline**—product replaced with different offering. Business development effort is low. Customer retention effort is low.

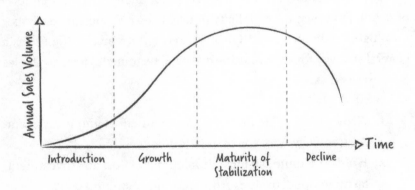

Figure 8: Product Life Cycle (Levitt 1965)

Understanding where the offering fits on this curve can assist in defining priorities for the business development effort across a portfolio of products or service offerings. Introduction and growth stages will require a lot more effort than the maturity or decline.

The Mysteries of Market Mapping

Market mapping is the process of interpreting and characterizing the part of the sales ecosystem that your company lives within—the market. In my experience, this analysis has a tendency to become hyper detailed, filling pages of spreadsheets and a multitude of charts. The amount of hours and cost can become prohibitive, especially for the start-up or small business.

I once undertook an exercise like this for a local start-up looking at the global mining industry. I spent two solid weeks collecting data and compiling a spreadsheet of planet wide mine sites and their statistics. Of course, this resulted in a highly complex dataset. It was so detailed that the CEO had to code an algorithm to interrogate it.

Luckily for them, I conducted this exercise free of charge. If they had been paying for someone's time, I don't think the application would have been half as appealing. A better use of my time would have been spent gaining a high-level understanding of the global industry and then talking to the people within it. You can't beat real time feedback.

Unless you are a multinational conglomerate with very deep pockets, I believe you must keep your market mapping simple. All you require is a broad analysis of the main constituents, enough to allow decision-making around industry, and segment priorities.

A simple market analysis involves the following steps:

Geography—which region does your business development responsibility cover? Whether it is a particular region within a single country, or a group of countries, the boundaries need to be defined.

Site Type—in what sort of site is your product or service going to be used? Hospitals, contaminated land, mines, factories, water treatment plants, lawyer offices, you need to be specific here.

Site Numbers—establish how many of the sites identified above are present in your geographical area of responsibility.

Market Size—consider how much money a site is likely to spend on your offering over the next three years. Average this number out across all the sites for a single year. The total of these figures is the market size that your company is operating within. If you are operating within multiple site types, do this for each and combine the total.

Market Share—think about how much market share you can realistically attain over the next year. Link it back to the planning hierarchy—what types and sizes of projects you are looking to win? How many competitors are out there? Will you be playing in a "blue ocean" with no sharks, or a red ocean full of sharks competing for your customers (Kim and Mauborgne 2005)? If your company is well established, your market share could be at 30 percent or more. If you are just starting out in a market with many competitors, 1-2 percent may be more achievable.

Available Market—using the formula *market share* x *market size = available market* provides a good indicator of where the opportunity for your offering is greatest.

Market research is often considered to be an overwhelming task, especially if you are expecting to collect millions of data points. However, utilizing market researchers on gig economy sites like www.fiverr.com can get you the specific site data for your region quickly and cheaply. A hundred dollars can get you a decent data set, listing the relevant sites within your region in the fraction of the time it would take you to source that information yourself.

Table 1 is an example of a simple analysis that you would conduct for each of the market segments that you are considering. It allows you to prioritize which segments to pursue. I'll use the following example to show how it works.

Jen is an experienced water engineering consultant with strong industry connections who has recently decided that she is going to start her own consultancy. She knows her services are in demand in both the water utilities and mining sectors. While she has contacts in both industries, she wants to know where she should be prioritizing her valuable business development time.

Using a freelance website, Jen requests all the water treatment plants and mine sites in her region. She estimates that the water treatment plants would be likely to require $50,000 of her services a year, while the mine sites would only need $10,000 per year. There are five water treatment plants and forty mine sites, so Jen created the following table:

Table 1: Market Analysis Example

Segment	Site	No. of Sites	$ per Year	Market Size	Market Share	Available Market
Water Utilities	Water Treatment Plant	5	$50,000	$250,000	25%	$62,500
Mining	Mine	40	$10,000	$400,000	5%	$20,000

While the mining segment has a larger market size, Jen determines that the number of competitors and her own network in the mining industry provides a market share of only five percent, whereas her work is well known and valued in the water utilities sector and, though the market size is smaller, she should be able to capture twenty five percent market share for water utilities.

This allows the available market to be calculated providing a very clear picture of where Jen's business development priorities should be focused. That is not to say that she would not seek opportunities in mining; this could be a longer-term strategic play. However, the immediate low hanging fruit is firmly within the water utilities segment.

Who Are Your Customers?

I remember starting my first day with an environmental services company as their state manager, a leadership and business development role that was outside my previous water-focused expertise. This was an exciting posting, and I was looking forward to building on the existing customer base. Enthusiastically, I sat down with the small team and asked the simple question, "Who are our customers?"

I was met with blank stares. I was falteringly told that they had once met with two or three companies, at which point they stuttered back into silence. Not the greatest of starts.

I recognized that there were two ways to respond. First, I could hang my head in despair, throw my hands in the air, and admit defeat. Or I could see this as an excellent opportunity to define what our ideal customers looked like. I could identify the low hanging fruit and take action. Of course, I chose action.

You may have the best product in the world and not be able to sell it. You need a willing buyer. The start-up scene is littered with the husks of companies that developed great products that nobody wanted. Effectively, it boils down to one simple fact.

If there is no *customer*, there is no *product* or *service*.

A company is nothing without customers who use its services or products. Each company has an ideal customer. The customer characteristics have to be defined. Each characteristic must be rated in terms of importance to your business and the direction of your future business development growth.

Defining Your Ideal Customer

First, picture what an ideal customer looks like. Who would you love to do business with? Give this some serious thought. Next, dive deep into the characteristics that make up the companies that you aspire to do business with. Ask yourself and the team the following questions to help define your perfect customer:

- Which industry does the company operate within?
- What size staff and annual turnover do they have?

- What work do they focus on?
- Are there specific products or services they need to be successful?
- What sort of people work there?
- Where are they located?
- How much will they spend on your product or service?
- Who are the decision makers around implementing your products or services?
- Who controls their budgets?

This is just the start. There will be many more questions that are unique to your industry and offering. For example, if you develop software solutions, you may need to know what operating system the customers use. In the environmental space, you may need to be aware of specific environmental legislation that relates to particular companies.

Forming a Customer Matrix

From your final list of questions, determine the top five to ten that are most important to your business offering. These will form the core attributes of your target customers, allowing potential customers to be easily identified and benchmarked. For easy comparison, embed these into the customer matrix shown in the table below.

Table 2: Example—Customer Matrix for Environmental
Consulting for the Mining Sector

Attribute	Ideal Customer	Customer 1	Customer 2	Customer 3
Annual Turnover	$3M +			
Company type: miner, contractor, support	All three			
Potential Service Spend	$100K +			
Projects with Environmental Sensitivity	Many			
Limited In-House Capability	No more than 1-2 in-house specialists			
Bureaucracy of Accounts Payable	Low			
Strong Social License to Operate	Yes			
Current Customer	Yes			

Filling in the matrix with existing customers gives you a good picture of who should be retained, and who shouldn't. It allows you to make a quick assessment of target companies to see whether they are a good fit for your business and whether time and resources should be allocated to their pursuit.

Use this matrix for new target customers, and for existing customers who both need to be serviced properly to be retained.

Customer Segmentation

Following creation of your customer matrix base, it's a good idea to look at customer segmentation. It is obvious that not all customers are created equal. Business developers only have a limited amount of time and resources. These must be spent on customers that give the best return.

Therefore, priority of effort must be defined. An easy method is to segment the list into three tiers. A quick way to determine priority level is to focus on both of the following:

- **Potential service spending**
- **Target customer's need for your company offering**

Let's take an environmental consultancy servicing the mining industry as an example. They specialize in managing and mitigating environmentally sensitive sites, particularly involving threatened ecosystems.

A company like this might define customer segmentation using *potential spending* on environmental consultancy services first, determined by their size and cash flow. Next, they might use the customer's number of environmentally sensitive projects to highlight the need they have for the company offering. This results in the three priority tiers:

- **Tier 1: $100,000/year spend and/or many environmentally sensitive projects.**
- **Tier 2: $60,000/year spend and/or some environmentally sensitive projects.**
- **Tier 3: $30,000/year spend and/or fewer environmentally sensitive projects.**

Looking through their customer list and placing them into the three tiers becomes a straightforward exercise.

This division can help you focus your effort on those companies that give you the highest return. Of course, tier 1 should be the given the highest priority. However, the lesser tiers also have the potential for significant revenue and must not be forgotten. Think about how much effort you will assign to each tier. How often will you contact your target companies? Will it be different for each tier?

I recognize that this approach can be considered too simple by some. But think of the customer segmentation as a guide to focus your business development effort.

There will be times where customer opportunities fall outside of this framework. In these instances, sit down with the team, discuss the likely returns and the effort needed to attain them. Use your customer segmentation to help shape the conversation. Work together to determine how to proceed. Perhaps there are unique strategic reasons to elevate a customer to tier 1?

Strategic Customer Targets

When looking at the strategic potential of customers, a great place to start is *Crossing the Chasm* by Geoffrey Moore. While this was written with technology adoption in mind, there are many parallels that can be drawn with business development. The book is particularly useful if you are relatively new to the market or introducing a new product or service.

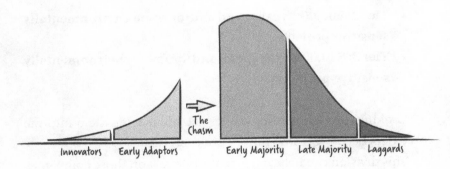

Figure 9: *Crossing the Chasm*, Moore, 1991.

Moore suggests that there are different stages of product adoption. Each stage has a transition point into the next. The hardest transition to cross is from *early adopters* to the *early majority*—in this case, smaller customers willing to take a risk on your services to the more mainstream and larger customer base. To *"cross the chasm"* between the two customer segments, you need to form a beachhead inside the *early majority*.

You need to secure a key reference customer who is highly regarded in your chosen customer segment or industry. You then use this association to gain more credibility with the often risk-averse customers of the *early majority*.

Moore uses the bowling pin analogy where you use your ball to strike one pin. This goes on to knock down the rest of the pins in quick succession. In our case, this means using your business development effort to capture one key reference client first before targeting the next.

Look at your completed customer matrix with a particular focus on your prospective customers. Which one of these has the strongest need for your company offering and the most industry influence? Is there a customer on your matrix whom others in the field follow?

This customer forms your beachhead into the early majority customer segment. An area of high growth and returns.

Let's take the mining industry in Australia as an example. Having one of the biggest players, like BHP or Rio Tinto, as your customer adds a huge level of credibility when talking to other mining companies. It is an opportunity to have your customers leave a conversation aware that your business is dealing with the industry leader. This provides a level of trust that your offering is valuable and that it may be worthwhile for them to engage with you too.

It is likely that the key reference company will be a longer-term strategic target. To reach it, the planning and effort must be made now. If you don't plan your beachhead assault now, you will never have the kudos of a key reference client in your portfolio.

In-House Relationships

It is critical to know who the main influencers and departmental contacts within your organization are, as well as gaining a good understanding of the way they operate. Internal relationships and alliances are essential when developing a durable foundation on which to base your business development action. Often, a joint effort with another team greatly enhances the company's offering to the customer. Market intelligence and contacts gathered by team members can make the difference between winning and losing opportunities.

Imagine having a potential customer with urgent technical questions that you are unable to answer. But you have made no effort to get to know the technical team. Your customer is screaming for assistance, but the team who could support you have priorities of their own.

A great working relationship with other teams means they are more likely to help you with your customers' requests. This allows you to respond quickly with the required detail, resulting in the customer receiving a much higher level of service. In turn, this gives you a stronger likelihood of winning or retaining their business.

Developing a relationship with the other teams in your company is not difficult. Keep them informed of what is going on. Let them know if large orders or projects are expected. Communication helps teams plan and prioritize their workload. It removes the unknown.

Ask their opinion on the subjects within their domain. Usually, this is beneficial to all parties involved. These teams value the interest shown in their work, and you learn from them at the same time.

I have worked for a couple of organizations with strong technical teams who rarely got to meet the customers. I found that regularly chatting with them about customer feedback and inviting them to specific customer meetings was highly valued. It gave the technical leaders an insight into how their work was received by the customer that they didn't get elsewhere. In turn, the customer benefits from the extra depth of knowledge at the table. This really helps in forming trust between the two disciplines, enabling each to appreciate the other better.

Engaging with teammates who have long industry experience may uncover customer contacts that you would not otherwise have known about. However, never underestimate the winning potential of your younger staff; you never know who they may bump into.

This happened to me as a new graduate member of an environmental team in London. I was having a beer at the local pub with some friends who also worked in the environmental industry. I was chatting to a friend of a friend and, inevitably, work came up in the conversation. It turned out that he worked for a large oil company and was looking for environmental consultants to undertake what he considered to be a small piece of work. We swapped details. The next morning, I went straight to my boss and discussed the opportunity. A few emails and calls later, we were tendering a multimillion-dollar contract.

Who Are Your Internal Stakeholders?

For a GDBD to succeed, it is vital to understand your organizational network. Who is responsible for what? Where can you go for additional market intelligence, support, or assistance? Who are the key internal influencers who get things done?

Take time to develop a stakeholder matrix for your organization, based on the skills, positions, and influences that will aid in the development of the business. A clear understanding of this landscape will allow you to take advantage of opportunities swiftly and efficiently. A simple stakeholder matrix will need to cover the following groups of personnel:

Subject Matter Experts—the technical specialists who know their subject inside out and are often a great source of market intelligence.

Team Leaders—it is essential to communicate with the team leaders during the sales process and again once opportunities have been won and need to be delivered.

Key Influencers—well-respected long-term employees or energetic newcomers, these are the staff members who others listen to and take seriously. Having key influencers as strong allies can help you to gain support for future business development initiatives.

Proposal and Quote Writing—personnel within the business unit who have time allocated to writing quotes and proposals or who are recognized as being particularly strong in this skillset. A close working relationship is required to ensure that large proposals and quotes have the best chance of success.

Market Sector Experts—great sources of business intelligence, leads, and contacts. Consult with these people to gain an understanding of the customer organizational chart and to secure personal introductions to key customer contacts.

Marketing Team—this group will be a primary source of leads. A strong working relationship must be developed to make sure messages and customer targeting are aligned. If communicated with clearly, this team can add significant weight to the top of your sales funnel.

Personnel with Revenue Targets—these are generally the leadership roles within the business. Understand their revenue targets and find out if they are willing to share resources in an effort to reach them. The GDBD can really be a savior to these individuals through the development of revenue opportunities, which can directly impact their end-of-year bonuses and the growth of their team.

Populating the matrix is relatively straightforward and should comprise the following columns shown on Table 3:

Table 3: Internal Stakeholder Matrix Table Template

Name	Role	Department	Interest	Influence	Action

Simply allocate high or low to the interest and influence columns and refer to figure 10 to determine how these should be **engaged.** This will enable each stakeholder to be plotted on the matrix below, allowing you to define their category and subsequent actions.

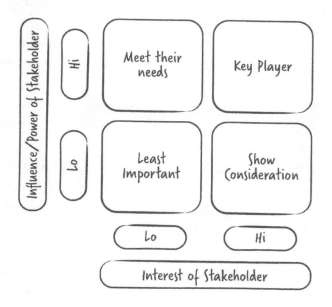

Figure 10: Stakeholder Matrix

The broad strategy associated with each stakeholder category are summarized below:

Key Player—with a high level of interest and influence, these stakeholders can have a strong impact on your business development efforts. The majority of your stakeholder engagement should be focused on this group. It can be beneficial to involve members in decision-making at times. *Action*: Engage and consult regularly.

Meet Their Needs—the high level of influence has the potential to make this group a valuable resource. They should be engaged and consulted on areas that are of interest to them. For example, on particular market segments or project types. *Action*: Increase their level of interest and move them to become key players.

Show Consideration—this group has high levels of interest but limited influence; as such, they should be considered potential supporters. There is opportunity to make use of their interest and involve them in low-risk areas around specific customers, products, or market segments. *Action*: keep informed and consult on interest areas.

Least Important—the low interest and influence levels gives this group the lowest priority with regards to engagement. *Action*: Keep informed through general communication and aim to increase interest levels over time.

Once the matrix is completed, assign time and resources to each of the key players. Learn their preferred communication styles and how best to connect with them. Consider the other stakeholder groups and think about how and when to engage them—perhaps a business development agenda item at team meetings or individual discussions on specific topics. Remember that each stakeholder is different. They all have a role to play in getting the company offering into the market and ultimately solving the customers' problems.

The most critical stakeholders must be added to the *tactical action plan* as part of the *aim* stage, which will be discussed in the next chapter of the book. The *tactical action plan* will systematize the contact and action with each stakeholder, making sure their engagement is not neglected.

Forming Internal Alliances

Take a step away from the business development capability for a moment. There will be people within the organization who have complementary skills and goals but who sit outside your normal sphere of operations.

This can take the form of teams with different offerings, willing to take a multidisciplinary approach to success. The ability to bid on projects with other teams really strengthens your proposal—or perhaps a customer account manager who knows that your offering aligns with their sector of responsibility and feels they can help get your foot in the door, using their account influence to increase your sales, and ultimately reach their targets quicker.

Many of these will have already been identified as key player stakeholders. Think about who these people and teams may be in your workplace. Consider how an alliance might work; it must be advantageous to both parties.

Think about how best to approach them. A simple coffee catch-up and a sharing of knowledge and opportunities may be enough to begin with. But if you are both working on proposals together, reflect on how the effort is to be shared.

It is important, however, to make sure these catch-ups are captured systematically in your *tactical action plan*; otherwise, it is easy for your business development agenda to get lost in the thousands of other priorities that each of these people have every day.

Business Development Resources

Prior to accepting a business development role, there must be clarity on what resources are being made available to develop the business. This can be divided into the following core resources:

Budget—how much money has been assigned to the business development function, and what are the allowances for marketing? This can become critical if the business development component is only one part of your role. How much time is expected to be spent on business development, and how much on the other tasks?

Personnel—discover what staff the business development function has been allocated, and define what their roles are. Identify which personnel outside the business development function have hours assigned to assist with administration, proposal writing, customer visits, customer relationships, quoting, etc.

Access to Marketing—work out who runs the marketing function within the organization, and how much access is available to their resources. Determine any guidelines and requirements around the marketing direction desired by the company. What are their policies on social media?

Access to Market Research/Intelligence—Does the company undertake systematic market research and intelligence that you can access? If they don't, think about where the intelligence for your industry could come from and ways to gain access to it. This could take the form of engaging an external provider, subscriptions to relevant trade journals, and papers or attendance to industry conferences and networking events.

Departmental Business Development Meetings—determine whether the wider team holds business development meetings with the relevant stakeholders, and if they don't, ask if they would they be willing to. This is a good indicator of the value that is placed on the business development activity within the unit.

Interdepartmental Business Development Meetings—find out if business development is systematically discussed across the organization. How do business units work together in pursuit of opportunities? Consider taking the lead in implementing a regular interdepartmental conversation.

A Seat in the Leadership Group—establish whether the business development function have a say in the leadership of the business. This is critical if the company is to adjust quickly to changes in the market and keep its offering relevant to the customer base. You will need to prioritize the leadership team as part of your stakeholder engagement and keep them informed on relevant opportunities and progress.

Having looked at the above resources, are you confident they will be enough to support the effort required to meet expectations? If there are gaps, think about where you can beg, borrow, or buy the additional assets required. Are there resources shared amongst other teams that you can borrow? Perhaps younger team members can assist. This can be a useful way for them to gain experience and skills in business development.

Some of the market research can be outsourced using the gig economy through websites like www.fiver.com or www.upwork.com. There are lots of options available that don't need full-time staff.

Gaining access to adequate resources may require a robust conversation with the leadership team to determine the level of support you need and why you need it. Remember that resources are only allocated if an adequate return on effort and cost is defined.

Make a case around why the resources you need add value to the business development process. Define how each one is going to increase revenue income. It can be as simple as using a junior member of staff to assist in writing first draft proposals, to free up more of your time to develop client relationships. Remember to make your case, detail who these clients are, and outline what projects they are likely to bring in.

External Environment

Having gained a good understanding of the inner workings of your organization, it is time to define the operational environment of the sales ecosystem. Where are the customers and competitors, and how does your company fit?

We have already completed a simple market analysis earlier to get an idea of market size and customers. The external environment is more than an analysis of the market. At the basic level, we want to understand the setting that our team, organization, and customers operate within. This includes the industry, geography, external stakeholders, and those competing with you for your customer base.

Operating Industry

In the context of the sales ecosystem, your industry comprises the habitat that your target customers operate within. Additionally, this includes their sources of influence. Starting with the broad industry, consider the following questions:

- Who are the visible influencers of this industry internationally, nationally, and locally?
- Which industry bodies are the most popular and the most active?
- Where do members of the industry go for information and advice?
- Which segments of the industry are most applicable to your company offering?

Taking the construction industry as an example, there are well-regarded individuals who regularly talk and interact at the industry level. They will be active on blogs, social media, webinars, and industry discussion panels.

Here in Australia, some of the construction industry bodies to investigate include the Australian Construction Industry Forum, Engineering Australia, and Institute of Architects, to name a few. If your company is focused on the engineering side of the industry, Engineers Australia would be an ideal place to start.

Ask yourself which influencers and organizations are key to the industry that you operate within. Answering these questions around your operating industry will begin to give a picture of the key influencers and most influential organizations. This information is essential in developing your *external stakeholder matrix*, which will be discussed in later sections.

Target Geography

Where in the world are you doing business? How does this impact your approach? This is usually straightforward to answer when you are operating within your home country. But a thick layer of complexity is added when the business is developing overseas.

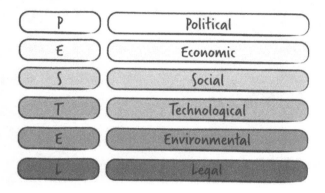

Figure 11: PESTEL Analysis (Kaplan et al, 2008)

For each geography in your portfolio, develop an overview of the broader environment that your sales ecosystem sits within. Determine how business is done there, what the culture is like, and how to navigate it. The PESTEL analysis is a simple tool that helps shape our thinking in this regard.

The PESTEL analysis covers the following:

- **Political**—what is the political environment like? Is the government stable, are there trade restrictions, and is corruption rife?
- **Economic**—is the economy of the area growing? Are companies thriving, and do customers have disposable income? Are the exchange rates favorable (particularly useful if you are importing/exporting products)?

- **Social**—is the population growing, and what are their attitudes to safety, health, and career? Are they socially aware?
- **Technological**—is new technology and innovation widely accepted and actively encouraged? Are there incentives in the advancement and introduction of new technologies?
- **Environmental**—what is the environment like? Does it suffer from harsh conditions, and is it protected properly?
- **Legal**—how robust is the legal system, and how strong is the focus on discrimination, consumer laws, and health and safety?

If you are operating within multiple geographies, the PESTEL can give a good feel for the differences. While coarse in its approach, it does get you thinking along the right lines.

Cross Border Culture

It is an all too common mistake to expect others to think and act the same way you do. Taking time to understand any differences in culture and behavior and considering approaches to bridge them is very worthwhile. For example, leading a business development campaign in Australia would take a very different form to one being conducted in Indonesia.

Social and hierarchical behavior can vary significantly from place to place. If the company operations are spanning multiple geographies and cultures, I recommend reading around the Lewis model to gain an understanding about how to navigate potential communication pitfalls. Lewis broadly divides the world's cultures into three communication styles—*linear-active*, *multi-active*, and *reactive*—and describes how each style behaves. A very brief summary of each style is provided in Table 4.

Table 4: Summary of Lewis Model Communication Styles
(from crossculture.com, 2015)

Linear-Active	Multi-Active	Reactive
Talks half the time;	Talks most of the time;	Listens most of the time;
Does one thing at a time;	Does several things at once;	Reacts to partner's reaction;
Plans ahead step by step;	Plans grand outline only;	Looks at general principles;
Polite but direct;	Emotional;	Polite, indirect;
Partly conceals feelings;	Displays feelings;	Conceals feelings;
Confronts with logic;	Confronts emotionally;	Never confronts;
Dislikes losing face;	Has good excuses;	Must not lose face;
Rarely interrupts;	Often interrupts;	Doesn't interrupt;
Job-oriented;	People-oriented;	Very people-oriented;
Sticks to facts;	Feelings before facts;	Statements are promises;
Truth before diplomacy;	Flexible truth;	Diplomacy over truth;
Sometimes impatient;	Impatient;	Patient;
Limited body language;	Unlimited body language;	Subtle body language;
Respects officialdom;	Seeks out key person;	Uses connections;
Separates the social and professional.	Mixes the social and professional.	Connects the social and the professional.

Each of the three groups can be applied to different parts of the world. The linear-active group comprises the English-speaking world—North America, Britain, Australia, New Zealand, and Northern Europe. The reactive group is located in all major countries in Asia, except the Indian subcontinent, which is a hybrid.

The multi-active group are more scattered and comprises Southern Europe, Mediterranean countries, South America, sub-Saharan Africa, Arab (and other cultures in the Middle East), India, Pakistan, and most of the Slavs. Bear in mind that these are generalizations, but understanding them can really help bridge communication across cultures.

The importance of understanding cultural differences became apparent to me in the first two weeks of starting a new role. I was reporting through to Singapore, and we had a huge variety of nationalities working in the same team. Experiencing some urgent technical issues with one of our customers, I tried to push things through quickly, outside of our regular operating process. To me, this seemed the obvious thing to do. Not so to the rest of the team. I met resistance. Moreover, they would tell me that they would help, but they didn't. It was infuriating.

Luckily for me, a great mentor of mine, Shirley Anne, introduced me to the Lewis model. I was operating as a linear-active whilst most of my colleagues were reactive. They weren't happy that I was circumventing the work process and, as reactives, they wouldn't confront me about it. As a linear-active, I was becoming impatient, and the logic of bending the work process seemed obvious to me.

Importantly, Shirley Anne helped me see that what was infuriating for me was also exasperating for the Singapore team. I gained insight into how the team members operated and adjusted my style and expectations to suit. Ultimately, a good outcome was reached for our customer.

External Stakeholders

When I started work as a state manager for a national asbestos removal company, I had very few contacts within that industry and, much to my surprise, we had no recurring customers in my geographical territory. While assessing the sales ecosystem, it became clear that the consultants who set up and oversaw projects for their clients needed a removalist contractor whose work reflected well on them. In turn, we, as the contractors, needed good consultants—the relationship went both ways.

I quickly identified a series of consultants whose work ethic mirrored our own. Thereafter, we began forging mutually beneficial relationships with them. This introduced us to projects and clients that we had no prior relationship with. In turn, we provided an additional source of jobs and the certainty of our professional service to the consultants. Both our revenues increased as a result. This taught me that alliances with key players in the market can have a strong influence on your success.

Take some time to really understand the market ecosystem. Who does what, and why? Who are the key players within your sales ecosystem, and how much influence do they have? Do any of these influencers align with your organizational mission and values, and is there a gap that can be filled in a way that benefits both parties?

Similar to the exercise for internal stakeholders in the previous chapter, a matrix can be developed for the stakeholders external to the company. A simple external stakeholder matrix will likely cover the following groups:

Industry Experts—technical experts with a strong positive reputation within the industry. Their opinion carries a lot of weight with industry groups and customers, often a great source of market intelligence, technical advice, and free marketing/referrals, if they value your company offering.

Key Influencers—not always the industry experts. These

individuals have a large industry-wide network and always know what is going on. They are an invaluable source of industry intelligence, and it is vital to have regular contact with at least one of these.

Consultants—providing specialist advice is a critical part of any industry, and consultants can be found for almost any topic or service. These can be customers themselves and are often the gateway to more prominent end users. Forming an alliance with a consultant who shares your principles and values your company offering is an excellent way to get access to specialist skills and a different stream of opportunities.

Government Departments—while not relevant to all industries, government departments provide valuable insights into industry trends and legislative requirements. They can make excellent recurring customers. Proving to these stakeholders that your offering follows best practice can make your company the benchmark from their point of view. If this becomes the case, government departments can become a good source of unofficial recommendations.

Industry Groups—most industries have groups, clubs, and peak bodies that form a hub for professionals to network and share ideas. Joining and attending these groups can provide up-to-date news on the industry and face-to-face access to customer contacts. Attending networking events and talks by these groups can place you in a relaxed setting, allowing you to form connections with people who would be difficult to contact during their busy working hours.

Using the methodology from the "In-House Relationships" section, generate a matrix from the stakeholders from the above categories. It will become apparent which ones to consider the *key players*. The strategies to nurture these stakeholders are also presented in the previous section. Ultimately, your alliance proposition must be beneficial to both parties. It must encompass a true win-win relationship.

Think about the external stakeholders in your industry. Are there any opportunities for alliances or closer working partnerships?

Competitor Analysis

Unfortunately, playing in a blue ocean market where your offering is the only option for your customers is extremely rare. There are always going to be other companies vying for your customers' money.

It is important to understand where, how, and why these competitors do business. Identify their strengths and weaknesses and how they compare to your own. Using a simple *competitor matrix* allows you to quickly assess your opposition and recognize where your advantages and disadvantages might lie.

Do a quick scan of your competitors and try to answer the following questions:

- What is their main offering, and how does it differ from yours?
- Why are they in business? Are they focused on maximizing profit or social legacy?
- What is their business and pricing model?
- Is the competitor winning more business—hiring and growing? What growth trajectory are they on? Are they a multinational company with enormous reserves or a tiny start-up scratching for resources?
- What does their team look like? Many staff across multiple disciplines, or a small number of highly specialized personnel? Do they have business development staff active in the market?
- Who are their key customers, and how loyal are they?
- How do they attract and retain customers? Do they have a proactive sales team hunting new customers? Are they marketing aggressively through social media or other channels?
- Do they hold significant market share?
- What is unique about their offering, and how is this different to your unique selling points?
- Which points of difference between the two companies can you successfully compete on?

The answers will provide enough information to start assessing the competition. A simple way to do this is through the creation of a competitor matrix. Generate a series of attributes based on the most important questions above. Next, populate the categories for your organization and each of your competitors.

Using a traffic light system to denote strength and weakness when compared to your company allows you to quickly visualize differences. For instance, RED signifies where they exceed your offering, while GREEN indicates where their offering is weaker. An example competitor matrix focused on a water consultant is provided in Table 5.

Table 5: Competitor Matrix

	Your Company	**Competitor 1**	**Competitor 2**
Product/Service	Water Consultant	Enviro Consultant	Water Consultant
Business Model	Specialized—mine dewatering, high fee	Quick, cheap, minimal reporting	Specialized modelling, high fee
Financial Resources	Medium	High	Low, one-man band
Market Share	20%	30%	5%
Growth	Strong	Strong	No Growth
Marketing Strategies	Word of mouth	Social media, event sponsors	Word of mouth
Strengths	Mining skillset Quality of outcomes	Fast reporting Low prices	Water modelling leader
Weaknesses	. . .	Quality of reporting	. . .

Once completed, the competitor matrix will provide a broad indication of the competitor's strengths and weaknesses in relation to your company. This will allow competitive messaging to be formed for marketing, and it will also inform any conversations in which customers bring up competitors' offerings.

The example competitor matrix in Table 5, while incomplete, gives insight into who the competitors are and how they operate. Perhaps the water consultancy in question needs to do more marketing. In addition, Competitor 2 has a very specific specialization and may be a good partner for a future alliance.

Importantly, the matrix can help guide decision-making around changes to your company offering. It may highlight a weakness that needs to be minimized or strengthened to be reinforced. The competitive landscape is a crucial part of the sales ecosystem, and any changes in competitor information should be fed back into the company immediately.

Assess Summary

The goal of the *assess* stage of the *triple A framework* has been to develop your thinking around the key elements of your company, offering, customers, and environment—all the parts of the sales ecosystem. It has also provided some tools to assist with visualization of the data.

Following along with the text and doing the exercises will provide a good understanding of your company, where it is placed in the market, and what needs to be done from a business development perspective to grow the business.

The next stage, *aim*, will take this information and use it to develop a series of robust plans to enable proactive, systematic *action* to grow existing customer revenue and gain new customers.

TRIPLE A: ASSESS–TOP TIPS

The *assess* stage of the *triple A framework* is focused on developing a deep understanding of your sales ecosystem.

—Having an awareness of your company and business unit vision and objective is critical. The intent of your business will act as a compass guiding your business development effort.

—Plotting your products and services on Porters Generic Strategies and the GE/McKinsey Matrix can give a quick indication of where they sit commercially. These also provide simple strategies for each.

—While essential market mapping does not need to be complicated or expensive, having a coarse market map helps direct your effort and should be refined through customer feedback and discussion.

—A business without customers is not a business. Define the attributes of your ideal customer. Use these to assess existing and future customers by developing a customer matrix.

—Choose your longer-term strategic customers carefully. They must have a position as a key reference that other customers in the market look up to. Getting one of these on to your active customer list will add credibility to your offering and open the door to new sales.

—While business development is mostly focused on activities outside of your organization, do not neglect the relationships in-house. Strong bonds with the other teams in your company can help you respond to customers' needs faster.

—Collaboration with other teams can result in presenting stronger proposals than you could achieve alone.

—The environment external to your company contains more than just your customers. Assessing your external stakeholders and competitors allows for a better understanding of where your business fits on the wider landscape of the sales ecosystem. Gaps in the market and potential alliances with others can be identified and considered to increase the value of your offering.

TRIPLE A: ASSESS—FURTHER READING

—For a great introduction around sales today, look no further than Dan Pink's book *To Sell is Human: The Surprising Truth About Persuading, Convincing, and Influencing Others*.

—Michael Porter's generic strategies are explored in more detail in the book *Competitive Advantage: Creating and Sustaining Superior Performance*.

—McKinsey has published some great insights on the GE/McKinsey Matrix at the website https://www.mckinsey.com/business-functions/strategy-and-corporate-finance/our-insights/enduring-ideas-the-ge-and-mckinsey-nine-box-matrix

—While written for acceptance of tech products, Geoffrey Moore's book *Crossing the Chasm: Marketing and Selling Technology Products to Mainstream Customers* provides excellent advice on identifying and securing strategic reference customers.

Business Example: Assess

We come back to the example at Weyland Consulting Services to see the shaping of the *assess* stage for a newly promoted technical employee.

Strategic Intent

Following your appointment as team leader, you immediately book a meeting with Sarah, your general manager. You have a clear agenda to determine the strategic intent of the company leadership. To keep the discussion focused, you detail the following three talking points:

- **Company Vision and Objective**
- **Business Unit Vision and Objective**
- **Target Expectations**

Sarah has a good understanding of the vision and objectives of WCS and how the environmental business unit aligns with these. However, she has not considered target expectations, and you have to develop these together, making sure that they are realistic and achievable. Knowing that more work is needed, you make sure that the expectations can be revisited after completion of a more detailed market analysis. Following the conversation, you review your notes and define the following:

Company Vision and Objective—WCS wants to be a one-stop provider of engineering solutions for global tier-1 customers and is chasing a strong global growth trajectory of 10 percent year after year.

Business Unit Vision and Objective—the company growth expectation is mirrored by the local environmental division. Sarah's intent for the division is to provide excellent specialist services to the projects within the WCS portfolio, while independently and sustainably growing their own customers and projects.

Target Expectations—Sarah has made it clear that the contaminated land team is considered a core growth area within the environmental division and that fairly aggressive targets are being set.

She is looking for $1,000,000 in revenue within the first year, with the aim of growing this progressively over future years. The team is regularly undertaking projects across the region and supporting interstate teams, and they reported revenue of $800,000 last year. You and Sarah agree that growth of $200,000 for this year is a realistic target.

Competitive Offering

Over the years completing projects for WCS, you have come to understand where the company services fit within the local marketplace. Using the competitive offering questions as a guideline, and following conversations with your team, you develop the following service statement specifically for the Contaminated Land Team.

> *Our Team offers specialist advice around investigating and managing contaminated land. By doing this, we manage the risk and legislative requirements for our clients. Our competitive advantage is the broad experience of the local team and the specialist expertise of our international experts that can be accessed to help solve the difficult niche problems sometimes experienced. Within the local market, we have greater proficiency than most of our competitors but also come in at a higher price point.*

Plotting the offering on Porters generic strategy reinforces the above statement (figure 12).

- **Scope: Narrow**—focused on customers with difficult and potentially costly contaminated land issues.
- **Source of Competitive Advantage: Differentiation**—offering specific niche services.

It is clear that the generic strategy for the team is one of *differentiation focus*—offering a specialized service in a niche market. This allows customer targets to be determined according to this niche.

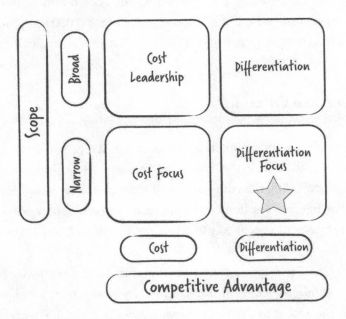

Figure 12: Porters Generic Strategy (2004) for Weyland Consulting

Market

To understand the market your team is playing in, you decide to define your specific geography as being centered on your local state, with a specific focus on the capital city and its surrounding area. You research land developments, aging mine sites, fuel sites, and heavy industry. This is checked with your understanding of where the team has had success in the past. It becomes clear that the mining and land development industries are the initial priority targets. The fuel station network sits as a longer-term opportunity.

Taking the mining segment as an example, you develop the following table detailing an approximate market size based on the number of mine sites and a likely spending limit of $50,000 per site, founded on your prior experience working on mining projects (Table 6).

Table 6: WCS Mining Market Example

Segment	Site	No. of Sites	$ per Year	Market Size	Market Share	Available Market
Mining	Mine	200	$50,000	$10,000,000	10%	$1,000,000
Land Development	. . .	. . .	. . .	. . .	. . .	. . .
Fuel Sites	. . .	. . .	. . .	. . .	. . .	. . .
Heavy Industry	. . .	. . .	. . .	. . .	. . .	. . .

A 10 percent market share consists of projects on twenty mine sites. This seems to be a realistic target to aspire to given WCS has a good footprint in the mining industry already.

Customers

Looking at the market composition, you develop an ideal customer profile before populating a customer matrix for each industry. For this example, we will look only at developing the mining matrix.

It is important that you pursue companies that are likely to spend on your team's services. So, you complete the profile based on mining companies that own and are operating assets that have a potential for contaminated land issues. In addition, they have limited capability to investigate and remediate these issues in-house. This shows a real need for your services.

Next, you identify likely customers and profile them on your customer matrix (a section of this customer matrix is presented in Table 7).

Table 7: WCS Customer Matrix Example

Attribute	Ideal Customer	Red River Mining	Compass Gold	Starlight Minerals
Annual Turnover	$20M +	$1B +	$100M	$20M
Company type—miner, contractor, support	Mine Operator/ Owner	Yes	Yes	Yes
Number of Mine Sites	2+	12	8	2
Potential Service Spend	$50K +	$600K	$300K	$50K
Projects with Contamination issues	Many	12	6	1
Limited In-House Capability	No More Than 1-2 In-House Specialists	1 Specialist	None	None

Attribute	Ideal Customer	Red River Mining	Compass Gold	Starlight Minerals
Bureaucracy of Accounts payable	Low	Medium	Low	Low
Strong Social License to Operate	Yes	Yes	Yes	No
Current Customer	Yes	No	Yes	No

From the small section of the matrix above, you determine that retaining Compass Gold as a customer is a high priority, as is actively pursuing Red River Mining, while Starlight Minerals should not feature highly on the priority list.

Internal Environment

In an effort to understand the situation within WCS Consulting, you continue to have conversations with Sarah and other members of the leadership team. It becomes clear that, while there is a business development budget, it is shared between all the functions of the environment division, and the split is not well defined.

You see this as a chance to define how many of the resources you can access. Drawing up a quick budget, you are able to secure funding for attendance at a number of local land development and mining events where you know many potential customers will be present.

In terms of time to be spent on business development activities, you decide your role is to be split evenly between leadership, project work, and business development activities, which allows thirteen hours a week to be dedicated to winning work. You know that this is particularly important when working in a consultancy where every hour is counted, allocated, and scrutinized.

In addition to utilizing the contaminated land team to assist in writing proposals, you discover that the environment division has two senior consultants with lots of bid-winning experience who can assist on the bigger proposals. A national sales team is also available for working on the large, country-wide, and international contracts.

The WCS core marketing team is based in the USA, and there is limited access to them. You see this as an opportunity to push your own marketing agenda in this region, particularly through the use of targeted LinkedIn posting.

Business development discussions about immediate opportunities take place on a weekly basis during the environment division leadership meetings. Resources are discussed with a focus on potential upcoming wins, as well as recent losses and market intelligence.

There is no specific business development meeting to discuss leads, marketing, or long-term opportunities, and you think that this could be an opportunity to instill a stronger business development focus on the environment division as a whole. You talk to Sarah about this gap, and she agrees to trialing the meeting and appoints you as coordinator and chair. As a result, you set the agenda and run these meetings—keeping them short, to the point, and on topic, to create value and allow them to become established over the longer term.

Understanding the local stakeholders proves to be a relatively quick exercise, and you identify the key players within the environment and other engineering divisions, particularly the construction teams. The general manager and the contaminated land service line leader in the USA also make the list. A small section of your local stakeholder matrix is shown in Table 8 below.

Table 8: WCS Local Stakeholder Matrix Example

Name	Role	Department	Interest	Influence	Action
Joseph C	CLM Service Line Leader	Corporate	High	High	Schedule Monthly Online Chat
Mary L	Team Leader Roads	Engineering: Infrastructure	High	Med	Monthly F2F Catch-Up
. . .	. . .	. . .	. . .	. . .	. . .

The populated local stakeholder matrix makes it easy for you to prioritize those key players you want to build internal alliances with.

You see real value in the larger infrastructure projects, which are often built on contaminated land or, at minimum, require an initial investigation. By creating alliances with the infrastructure division teams, you hope that your team can assist with proposals, project design, and execution on the larger projects. This allows your team's skillset to be integrated into projects right from the beginning. You know that, by working together, you and your team can help strengthen the infrastructure division's offering to their clients and develop a new stream of project work.

External Environment

Having defined the market that the WCS contaminated land team is playing within, it is clear that the two main industries being pursued are mining and land development.

Taking the mining industry as an example, you investigate the local influencers and industry bodies. You discover that the local mining club holds regular networking events and industry talks, giving access to many of the influencers within the local ecosystem.

There are also a number of local miners who regularly post

industry information and commentary on LinkedIn and their own blogs. You plan to interact with these people by commenting on their posts and engaging with their blogs, particularly on subjects involving contaminated land issues that your team can help solve.

You have a couple of colleagues who are now working with the mining companies directly, and who are excellent sources for trends and activity within the industry. These informal connections are a brilliant source of mining knowledge, and you plan to schedule an informal chat on a quarterly basis.

A number of Perth-based contractors specialize in the removal of contaminated soils and work on projects across the local area. You have worked with a couple of these specialists on projects in the past, and you value the work ethic of two in particular. There is a real advantage in fostering alliances here, as their work would reflect well on your team. Perhaps there will be an opportunity to bid on future projects together, presenting a more complete offering to the customer.

Inevitably, there are other providers of contaminated land services in the local area. While you know who most of these are, you feel it is still worthwhile to complete a *competitor analysis* to understand where the competition sits in comparison to your own team. A small part of this analysis is presented in Table 9.

Table 9: WCS Competitor Analysis Example

	WCS Consulting	BFG	Dragon Environmental	...
Product/ Service	Multi-discipline engineering	Multi-discipline engineering	Contaminated land only	...
Financial Resources	High	High	Low	...
Market Share	Med	Med	High	...
Growth	Steady	Low	High	...
Marketing/ Sales	International focus	Rely on existing relationships	Play on strong local reputation	...
Strengths	Project delivery and multi disciplines	Very strong relationships	Affordable niche offering	...
Weaknesses	Some internal siloes	Not interested in work beyond existing relationships	Don't have the resources to undertake very large projects	...

Once completed, you see that the team's differentiator is the larger projects that they can work on with the wider WCS team, something that most of the competition cannot access without partnering with potential competitors—a valuable insight.

WCS Assess Summary

Having completed the *assess* stage of the *triple A framework*, you have a good understanding of the sales ecosystem. Planning the direction of your business development efforts can be aligned with the WCS intent.

You know who your allies within the organization are and who you should be talking to about business development. The focus industries have been identified, and you have made a first pass to understand the customers.

The competitive landscape has also been clarified, which places even more value on the internal alliances available to your team. You are now ready to use this assessment to shape the business development direction into a series of structured plans that will define the future effort.

TRIPLE A: AIM

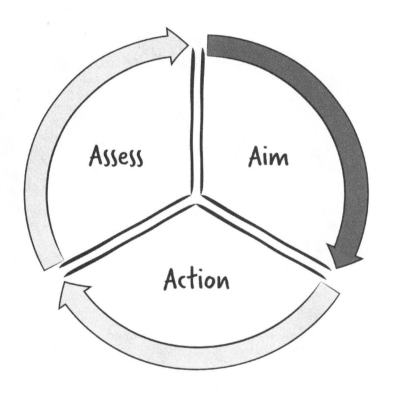

When undertaking business development for the first time, it opens up a world of possibilities. There are so many potential customers and opportunities that it can be difficult to know where to begin. This sense of being overwhelmed can cause procrastination and inaction—or an unstructured pursuit of opportunities, with no strategic consideration. Both are problematic and result in underperformance.

Your business development effort must be aimed in the right direction. You need a plan that aligns with the company purpose and the direction previously defined in the *assess* section. Most importantly, the plan should provide a framework for simple execution and quick opportunity assessment. It needs to foster action, not hinder it.

The effort required during the assessment stage is critical for defining the plan, and you will need to refer back to your notes to make sure the planning accurately reflects your findings around customers, markets, and stakeholders.

Now is the time to *aim* and plan your future business development effort.

Prioritize Your Effort

As a new business development professional, you come at the role full of energy and with the drive to win. Beware—it is easy to fall into the trap of chasing opportunities as soon as they appear, without any regard for their return, strategic importance, or likelihood of success. A lot of time can be wasted on the pursuit of a large, shiny-looking prospect, only to find that it does not quite line up with the company offering, direction, or intent.

In the previous section, customers were assessed and ordered into tiers. Now we need to go one step further to prioritize and document the future effort into a plan of action.

Mine the Gold You Already Have

Business development is often considered to be synonymous with sales. While increasing sales does form a core part of the role, the aim of a business developer is to develop the business. This involves looking for new customers, new markets, strategic partnerships, and new offerings. But there are so many opportunities, it can be difficult to know where to start focusing your efforts.

A model that can be used to frame your initial thinking is the Ansoff Matrix. This allows you to plot your products and service lines on the matrix below, using two axes, markets and products/services, divided into *existing* and *new*.

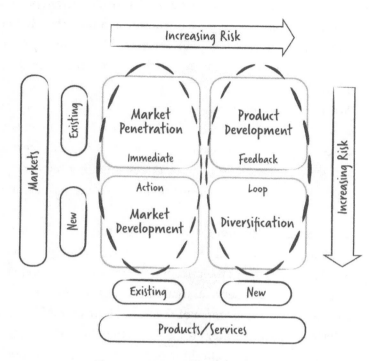

Figure 13: Ansoff Matrix (2015)

The Ansoff Matrix presented in figure 13 allows you to determine your broad strategy and gives an indication of where to start focusing your efforts.

A good rule is to begin where there is the lowest risk, extending the risk profile as you firm up your revenue foundation. The matrix can be used to help identify the low-hanging fruit, *immediate action*, to focus on. It also displays those actions to consider once a *feedback loop* with the market and customer base has been established. This allows the GDBD to adjust the company offering built on market and customer feedback.

Based on the matrix above, business development effort should be prioritized in the following order:

1. **Market Penetration (Lowest Risk)**—provide current products to the existing customer base. These customers already know your company and use your services. Continue expanding your existing offering amongst those who understand and appreciate it.
2. **Market Development**—provide existing products to new markets. This takes your knowledge from the existing customers and products and applies it to new customers and markets. For example, a transport engineering team may be able to push their services into developing roads for the mining industry.
3. **Product Development**—develop new products for existing customers. Using your relationships with existing customers and the knowledge of their needs can enable the development of new products and services that may solve additional problems for them. A good example of this is outdoor brand Patagonia, offering their customers tough-wearing climbing clothes in addition to their best climbing hardware (Chouinard 2006).
4. **Diversification (Highest Risk)**—create new products for new customers. Using the knowledge and experience of developing new products for existing customers can give insight into applying it to new customers. This should only be considered once a robust feedback loop within the market has been in place for some time, to enable diversification decisions to be based on real market data.

The Ansoff matrix (2015) highlights a key lesson for any budding GDBD: **start mining the gold you already have.**

I heard this fantastic analogy whilst listening to an interview where Tiffani Bova, a senior executive with Salesforce, was a guest speaker on the *Business Made Simple* podcast. It really struck a chord with me.

During the days of the gold rush, when a prospector got lucky and struck gold, he wouldn't just get up and walk to the next mountain.

He would start mining the vein that he had already uncovered.

The same is true for business development. Start with your vein of gold—your existing customers—and work from there. They already know and like your service, your team, and your offering— they keep coming back. There is a level of goodwill here that makes it easier to target this group first. This goodwill can also help you gain references and referrals and circulate success stories, which, in turn, can help open doors to your new customers.

The second half of the matrix, which is centered on product development and diversification, can only be explored once an adaptive feedback loop has been established between the market, the customer base, the GDBD, and their company. Only then is enough information being absorbed to make new product development a successful undertaking.

When you do get to the product development and diversification phases, Jim Collins and Morten T. Hansen provide some excellent advice in their book, *Great by Choice: Uncertainty, Chaos, and Luck— Why Some Thrive Despite Them All*. They suggest that you don't go all-in with a new or diversified product, but instead conduct small trials with products, which have controlled costs. Repeating these small trials will allow you to learn which products are worth the effort. Do not bet the whole company on a new diversified product offering.

If you see a gap in the market for a new service or product, use this advice and consider how you can conduct a small, relatively risk-free, trial of your idea. Present this to the leadership for approval. This has a much higher chance of being accepted. If it works, the new offering can be grown from there. If it fails, document what has been learned and move on.

Key Customer Targets

As discussed previously, the Ansoff Matrix makes a clear prioritization of existing customers first. However, a successful GDBD should also begin developing the market beyond the existing customer base.

Existing products and services must be offered to new customers in order to grow business revenue. Using the information gathered so far, your key customer targets can be defined and assessed. The key customer targets should be divided into three categories and prioritized as follows:

1. **Retention**
2. **Short-Term Acquisition**
3. **Long-Term Acquisition**

The target priorities are summarized in the customer acquisition hierarchy, displayed in figure 14. This should be treated as a guide for the planning process, as there will inevitably be strategic long-term acquisitions that will require higher levels of priority and ongoing effort.

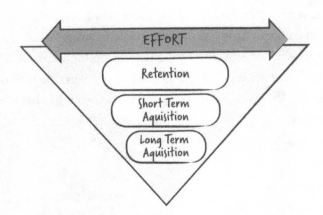

Figure 14: Customer Acquisition Hierarchy

Retention customers are those who are already buying your service or product and contribute significant annual income to your company. These are paying customers who are already champions of what you do. They provide a foundation of revenue that can be built upon and should not be allowed to erode. As such, they need to be nurtured with the aim to not only retain their business, but to increase the business that they do with you.

Pull out the customer matrix developed in the *assess* section and make a list of those top existing customers who make up 30 to 50 percent of your annual revenue. Next, look at the existing customers who are likely to achieve significant growth over the next one to three years. This segment will have the resources to spend more on your offering and can grow with you. These two groups should be tagged as first priority.

Your second priority should be new customers who have a burning need for your service and easy access to whoever makes the decisions. They should have enough resources to be able to afford your offering. These fall within the *short-term acquisition* category. These can be considered low-hanging fruit and should be approached with some urgency. Pull out the customer matrix again and determine which potential customers fit this category, labeling them *second priority*.

Your third priority is the long-term acquisitions. This group is formed from potential customers who have strong strategic potential but may require more effort to bring on board. Perhaps they have the potential for significant spending or a strong industry reputation.

Often, these organizations have a lot of bureaucracy, and it can be difficult to get in front of the decision makers. These require immediate effort, but with a longer-term reward in mind. Look at the customer matrix and find potential customers who fit this description and allocate them as *third priority*.

To summarize, prioritize your customers as follows:

- **First Priority**—existing customers who make up the top 50 percent of your revenue or have strong growth potential.
- **Second Priority**—new customers with a strong need for your service and who are relatively easy to access. They must be in a position to afford your offering.
- **Third Priority**—strategic customers with strong strategic value but who are harder to access.

I recognize that the above prioritization is a generalization and may not work for every industry or offering. If this is the case for you, use this framework as a tool to build your own set of prioritizations. However you do it, prioritizing your customers to allow efficient allocation of effort is a critical part of the planning process.

It is likely that the list you develop may be large and a little overwhelming. You may be concerned about where you will find the resources to hit all of these key customer targets at once. What worked for me is allocating ten to each category as a starting place. Aim to regularly add additional targets over time. Remember the saying "Life's a marathon, not a sprint." The same is true of business development.

Revisit Target Expectations

Having completed the initial internal and external assessments of your company and its place in the market, you need to consider how the targets set by leadership are going to be achieved. What does the average sale look like for your business? Think about this impartially, take out emotion and optimism, and be conservative. Once you have the number, determine how many sales are required to meet the budget.

Divide these sales into retention customers and acquisition customers. How many new customers do you need to get on board every month to meet targets, and is this manageable? How much time will this require, and are there resources to cover this? If there are, great, time to get after it.

If resources are not readily available, then you will need to think about how to achieve the targets in a different way. Perhaps there are different projects or customers to pursue that will bring in greater revenue. Are you focusing on the right products and customers? Is there a large potential customer who you will need extra assistance to access? Check your assumptions and talk it over with your team.

Now you are ready to begin the hard work.

Five-Minute Marketing

Understanding the sales ecosystem surrounding your company and having a list of priority targets is essential. But you need to be able to connect the company offering to the customer. Promoting your product is critical in keeping your sales funnel full of leads. Before the sales planning can begin, you need to consider what marketing tools are available so that you can incorporate them into your systematic plan.

If your company has people in a marketing role, they should be identified as *key stakeholders* on your stakeholder matrix. Make sure a relationship is developed and that you understand what they are doing, how they are doing it, and, most importantly, why. Use this team to help target your priority customers. If the marketing function is focused on other parts of the business or does not exist within your company, then ultimately marketing will fall to you. This section provides a summary of some of the marketing options available.

When a customer interacts with your brand outside your normal day-to-day operations, this is called a customer touch point. For example, browsing your website for product information. There is a standing marketing maxim that you must have seven or more touch points with a potential customer before they trust your brand enough to buy from it. In order to do this effectively, sales and marketing departments must work and communicate closely to craft messages and approach customers in a coordinated way.

As is pointed out, in the book, *The Challenger Sale: Taking Control of the Customer Conversation* by Matthew Dixon and Brent Adamson, these two functions often fail to work together. Sales success is dependent on having symbiotic sales and marketing teams. Marketing should be generating customer touch points, leads, and opportunities that allow the business development teams to follow up in person and develop further. Marketing and sales should be talking the same talk and promoting the same message.

In many instances, particularly in smaller firms, a GDBD will be looking after both sales and marketing. Regardless of the size of your company, it doesn't hurt to do some marketing yourself, especially today, when there are lots of low-cost opportunities to get your brand out to market.

Before you start, you need to understand your company message and the unique selling points of your products and services. I recommend reading *Building a Story Brand*, where Donald Miller suggests framing yourself and your brand as a mentor for guiding your customer through a journey to solve their problems.

He advises that you make the customer the *hero* of the story, not you or your brand. How will your customer's journey be benefited by using your product, and what will their success look like? Using the concept of story branding will make the articulation of your company message much clearer and more relevant to your target customer base.

The goal of five-minute marketing is to develop an easy system of generating brand touch points with your customers. Ideally, these should be low cost and require minimal time investment. Taking a handful of five-minute blocks a day to invest in recurring marketing will get your customers thinking about you.

Below is a list of possible touch points between your company and your customers. Each of these has the potential to remind your customer of the value of your brand and offering. Each is an opportunity to highlight your customer as a hero. Make a note of those that are relevant to your situation, as they should be incorporated into the planning, which is detailed later in this chapter.

Five-minute marketing touch points can include any of the following categories:

Social Media: LinkedIn—deceivingly simple and often free, social media is an excellent way to get your message out there. Regularly posting information that offers value to your customers, and interacting with customer and industry groups, is a good way to raise market awareness. It is critical to keep your message relevant and on point so that your potential customers can understand how your offering will help them on their journey.

LinkedIn is generally the best platform from a professional standpoint, and I would recommend this as a first point of call particularly when focusing on business-to-business sales. Beware—cultivating social media can be a time sink and must be carefully managed.

Social Connections—social connections are often overlooked when it comes to business development. It is amazing how many social connections you create throughout your working life that are either in the same or ancillary industries. Make time to catch up with these people and talk shop. They can be a great source of market information, leads, and opportunities.

SEO and Website—search engine optimization is the art of optimizing your company website so that it appears first when potential customers are searching for your services online. With the world becoming more digitally-focused, having good SEO can make a real difference in the competition for customers.

It is unlikely that this is something you can do on your own; a specialist company may need to be engaged. Make sure that they provide a monthly update on progress and that the business development team is engaged in discussions around content and messaging.

Advertisements: Digital—if you know your customer demographic, digital adverts can be a good way to inform the market about new products or offerings. It is more expensive than social media, so it is important that the success of any campaign is measured to determine value for money.

Advertisements: Print—given the explosion of digital media, print advertising is unlikely to yield decent results for most industries. In my opinion, money is best spent elsewhere.

Tradeshows—attending tradeshows for niche markets and industries can be an excellent way to interact with the primary figures within that industry. The jury is out as to whether paying for a stand at these events is good value for money. However, the networking can be a gold mine of contacts and information.

Industry Association Membership and Sponsorship—membership and sponsorship can be an affordable way to get to know the key players within a specific industry or market. Regular attendance is required to develop the necessary relationships and get known for what you do.

Event Sponsorship—depending on the event, sponsorship can be a good way to get your brand in front of a niche audience. However, there is often a significant cost involved with this; make sure there is an opportunity to talk a bit about your company and to enable a better return on your spending.

Email—email is often perceived as the easiest form of communication in today's world. If crafted properly, it is a good way to make first contact with a new prospective client. Email will be more successful if your customer has already been exposed to your brand and message through some of the other touch points above, as it means you are not going in cold.

Be careful—emails can be easily misread. Your message must be clear and succinct and not be misconstrued as spam. Some ways to avoid this are to make your emails personalized to the recipient; do not copy and paste large chunks of information into the body of the email or add attachments. A short, simple introduction to your service, its advantages, and why you would like to follow up is enough. More than three sentences may be too much.

If you are working in different geographies, you may need to utilize different communication styles. Refer back to the Lewis Model in the earlier "Cross Border Culture" section for some guidance on things to consider.

Phone Calls—phone calls are an excellent way to begin forming a relationship with your customers. While not as personable as a face-to-face, this method can be essential in creating a connection and building trust.

Face-to-Face—while meeting with your customer is the most time consuming of the touch points, it is the best way to build trust and connection. Make sure you have something interesting and relevant to discuss so you do not waste their time. In my experience, one-to-one builds rapport, and two-to-one is a great way to introduce a technical specialist who can provide your customer with deeper insight.

Presentations—a presentation is a perfect way to impart something interesting to your customers. This must not be a sales presentation; rather, focus on a topic that offers knowledge and value to the customer in their day-to-day working life. Use this as an opportunity to build trust in your company and to cement credentials as a specialist in the field. On a side note, your customer's time is precious; make sure the topic is engaging and tailored to your audience.

Training—organize training to teach your customers about your particular niche and what it means for them. As a specialist, it is easy to forget that what seems obvious to you and your colleagues is often unknown to your customer base. This is an ideal opportunity to impart useful knowledge, cement a reputation as a specialist, and get some valuable face-to-face time with several customers at once.

In some circumstances, you can even get paid for it.

Consider the list of potential touch points and choose those that are relevant to your customer base. Which of these can you fit into your current work schedule? Which will help get your brand out there? Of course, social media, if used purposefully, jumps out as being the ideal first point of call. I present a practical LinkedIn methodology in a later chapter. Calling and connecting with customers is also a great way to spend five minutes of your marketing time. Whichever you choose will form the basis of the marketing activity that will be used to systematically fill your sales funnel.

Remember, sales and marketing need to work together. As a GDBD, it is up to you to make sure the messaging aligns between the two. Consistency of your message is critical to the perception that the market, industry, and customer informs your brand, company, and offering.

The Three Plans

Having completed an assessment of the company and the sales ecosystem that it resides in, it is easy to get carried away and start trying to do everything at once, achieving nothing. Despite having prioritized customers and defined your offering's unique differentiators, your enthusiasm will only get you so far. A systematic approach is essential if you want to start getting repeatable results.

The strategic intent and sales ecosystem assessment provide an excellent foundation on which to form a systematic and action-oriented business development plan. I really wanted to name the action section *"Aggressive,"* but I thought it might give people the wrong idea. Former Navy Seal, Jocko Willink, says it best in this quote from his podcast:

Rather than passively waiting to be told what to do, default-

aggressive leaders proactively seek out ways to further the strategic mission. They understand the commander's intent, and where they have authority to do so, they execute.

Effective business development cannot be achieved by sitting at a desk waiting for the customer to call. It requires daily effort by the GDBD to get into the market, to talk to customers, and to feedback the findings to the company leadership. Daily marketing activity leads into the sales funnel.

This, in turn, requires daily action, to turn leads into opportunities and then opportunities into sales. It never stops—the continuous cycle needs continuous effort. The effort needs to be directed in a way that keeps it working toward the goals of the business.

That is a lot of action and activity to stay on top of. In an ever-changing day where customers, opportunities, and leads are all competing for your time, there must be a system. A plan is required that outlines a system of prioritized action. This allows you to approach your customer base in line with your goals and prevents any customers and opportunities from being forgotten. The following section will lead you through the process of developing simple, yet effective, systemized plans to focus your business development activity.

Introducing the Three Plans

The core of the *aim* stage centers on a hierarchy of three plans, presented in figure 15.

Figure 15: Three Plan Hierarchy

1. **Strategic Plan**—the *strategic plan* contains the overarching goals and intent of the company. There will only ever be one of these plans in existence at once.

2. **Operational Plan**—the *operational plan* covers the goals and focus areas of the business development function. This may form part of a broader business unit plan. There should be a different operational plan for each area of operation. For example, though business development managers in Florida and Alaska will be following the same company direction and intent laid out in the overarching strategic plan, they should each have a separate operational plan that captures the local differences in the industry and market.

3. **Tactical Action Plan**—this daily use plan executes on the operational plan, identifying daily actions for the business developer.

It is not necessarily the role of the GDBD to develop all three plans. This will depend on the company size and structure. At a bare minimum, the GDBD must have input into the operational plan. It is critical that they have ownership of the tactical action plan.

Take care when developing these plans, as they shape the direction of the business development activity and, ultimately, the growth of your business. Use the data collated in the previous *assess* stage to aim your efforts in a direction based on evidence and opportunity, not gut feel.

Strategic Plan

The strategic plan is formed from the overarching strategy for the entire business. If you work for a multinational company, the strategy for your division may be guided by global business. This highlights the overall direction of the business and the priorities to be pursued. If you are working for a smaller business where no strategy is in place, talk to the leadership about either developing one or providing the detail around the key points of interest.

The key points of interest for the GDBD to consider are:

Purpose—what is the company there to do, and why is it doing what it does? This can be used during client conversations and marketing messaging, to let the customers engage with the larger intent behind the company.

For example, working for a company that provides environmental monitoring equipment, I defined the purpose as "supporting environmental monitoring excellence, enabling positive action in protecting our natural environment." Bringing this up in conversation really resonated with existing and prospective customers mirroring shared values, allowing trust to form.

If you are having trouble articulating or defining the purpose of your organization, I suggest reading *Start with Why* by Simon Sinek. This will provide the tools to really dig deep into the purpose of your company.

Consider the following:

Vision—what is the long-term vision of the company? What will it look like in five to ten years' time and, importantly, how will this shape the future customer base? Understanding this allows the business development activity to be aligned with the long-term goals of the company.

For example, take an engineering consultancy that articulates their long-term objective as moving from transport infrastructure as their main project base to obtaining a large mining project portfolio.

This enables their business development team to focus some of their energy on longer-term customer and project opportunities in the mining sector.

Mission—the company mission defines what the company does and how it does it. For example, a technical company might have a mission to provide the highest quality flow data for their customers, through technical superiority, instrumentation design, and manufacture. Defining this mission allows the company's sales and marketing messages to be aligned, to show that you walk the talk in what you do.

Financial Goals—what are the immediate and long-term financial goals of the company, and how does your business development effort support these? This information is important when prioritizing customers and making decisions around opportunity pursuit.

It should also make clear the acceptable pricing strategy, though this will differ between various geographies and industries. These financial goals must align with the wider company context.

Growth Areas—where are the intermediate and long-term growth areas expected to be? This information is critical to make sure that your business development effort aligns with the growth expectation of the company. How is growth going to be achieved? Consider the Ansoff Matrix here. New products, services, or customers?

For example, if the company BuildingPro was looking to grow in the residential housing market, the GDBD would need to align with the internal engineering specialists and start exploring residential housing opportunities. This doesn't mean that other opportunities wouldn't be explored, but priority should be placed, and time allocated, to pursuing the prioritized areas of growth.

Key Customers—who do the leadership team consider to be the key customers of the company? This information is gold, as key customers are usually the highest yielding customers with the strongest connection. Robust relationships and trust in your offering are assets that already exist here. It should not be too difficult to use these assets as leverage to fill your sales funnel.

To give you an idea of how this might look, consider this example. The new business developer at BuildingPro understands that the local company Open Homes is considered a key customer. After a little discussion with their internal stakeholders, a relationship with the main account manager for Open Homes is discovered. This enables the business developer to be introduced to some of the main decision makers in Open Homes, which then assists the business developer to build relationships of their own—a great start to their business development journey.

Customers that closely align with your concept of an ideal customer should also be highlighted here, tying in with the previously identified growth areas and the priority pursuits.

Once the main components of the strategic plan have been uncovered, it is worthwhile writing them down for future reference. Use the information gained in the *assess* chapter to provide even more context. I always have a copy of the strategic plan on the wall above my desk for reference. This lets me do a quick check-in to make sure the business development activities are on point in the context of the overall company direction and expectations.

If you are not sure of the best way to present this information, there are plenty of great examples online and in business leadership literature. An example of a simple plan, which I have used on numerous occasions, is presented below (figure 16). This can be a useful place to start. However, I recognize that every business is different, so feel free to amend and change the information as your needs dictate. For maximum impact, keep the plan simple and short, ideally to one page, where a quick scan with the eyes is enough to gain an understanding of the central intent.

EXAMPLE STRATEGIC PLAN

Purpose

Brief Company Purpose.

Vision

Short statement regarding the company vision,
highlighting those pieces relevant to your offering and
position. Aspirational in nature.

Mission

Succinct mission statement. More immediate in timeframe.

Revenue Target and Relevant Year

Revenue Target Composition (e.g., Target for each Industry)

Key Differentiator: Spell this out

Growth Areas: Define these

Key Customers: Defined and listed

Figure 16: Example Strategic Plan

Operational Plan

The strategic plan can now be used to determine the more granular
goals and priorities of the business development effort. These should

be compiled into a one-page operational plan. This takes the company-wide strategy and direction and applies it to the particular industries and markets within the GDBD's sphere of responsibility.

At a minimum, it should detail revenue targets, quoting targets, key industries, and actions. The actions must be measurable. Details of the measurable KPI should accompany each action.

A model framework is presented below to be adapted for your particular circumstances.

1. **Mission**—adapt the company mission to apply to your unique region and areas of responsibility.
2. **Targets**—detail the targets for revenue, volume of quoting, and number of business development meetings and calls. Do not fall into the trap of detailing too many targets, as this can confuse the priority of effort.
3. **Customer Experience**—define how you want the customer to engage with and experience your offering. This will shape how you approach customers and your internal delivery teams.
4. **Marketing**—which marketing tools are going to be used in support of the actions above? Detail social media plans, any specific events, and launches, etc.
5. **Existing Market Segments**—detail the key goals, targets, and actions for this segment of your customer base.
6. **New Market Segments**—new market segments may be longer-term goals and actions that are unlikely to yield immediate results but tie in with the growth aspirations of the company.
7. **Projects**—define projects specific to your team for the coming year. These could include development of the company website, marketing materials, or project references.
8. **Collaboration**—feature internal stakeholder alliances to enable smooth collaboration in any joint actions needed.

There are many examples of sales strategies to be found. The example presented in figure 17 is simple and succinct, capturing enough detail to be relevant, with priorities easily understood. I cannot say it enough—mold and adapt this to your own specific set of circumstances.

EXAMPLE OPERATIONAL PLAN

Mission

Detail the mission as it pertains to this specific market and industry.

Targets: Add monthly revenue and quoting targets at a minimum

Theme	Segment	Goal	Actions	KPI
Customers	Customer Experience	*Market Recognition of Customer Service*	Detail Actions	KPI for each action
	Marketing	*Inform Market of our complete offering*	Detail Actions	KPI for each action
Existing Markets	Segment #1	*Add Goal*	Detail Actions	KPI for each action
	Segment #2	*Add Goal*	Detail Actions	KPI for each action
New Market	Segment #3	*Market Penetration*	Detail Actions	KPI for each action
Projects	Project #1	*Add Goal*	Detail Actions	KPI for each action
	Project #2	*Add Goal*	Detail Actions	KPI for each action
Collaboration	Stakeholder Group #1	*Add Goal*	Detail Actions	KPI for each action
	Stakeholder Group #2	*Add Goal*	Detail Actions	KPI for each action

Figure 17: Example Operational Plan

Tactical Action Plan

One of the hardest aspects of business development is making sure that the level of effort remains high. Additionally, this effort must remain aligned with the strategy and intent of the company you represent. The level of activity is on you, as discussed in the very beginning of this book; taking action is a defining trait of a GDBD. Maintaining systematic effort is where the third plan, the tactical action plan, provides assistance.

Of the three plans, this is the one that should be referred to, annotated, and updated every day. The plan systemizes the outcomes of the assessing, strategizing, and planning into a series of daily actions. Much like the sales ecosystem that the company resides in, the tactical action plan is a living system that evolves every day.

The following section will provide advice on setting up the tactical action plan in line with your targets and intent. It will also explain how to use the plan to systematically drive activity every day.

Tactical Action Plan Setup

The overall purpose of this plan is to systemize your business development actions. Daily use of the plan should be a guide of who to contact, when and in what order of priority. To do this effectively, it must be set up in a way that makes it easy to use and understand. At a minimum, it should hold enough information to provide customer priority, history, and most importantly, a prompt to action.

Many companies spend an inordinate amount of money on a complex customer relationship management system. But off-the-shelf systems try to be everything to everyone and can often have too much functionality, too much complexity, and no way to truly incorporate the company goals or intent. A simpler way to track this information is on a shared setup in a user-friendly, well-known system like Excel,

Google Sheets, or something similar. The actual format will differ between companies, but at a minimum, it should contain the following columns for each contact, opportunity, and lead:

1. **Due**—probably the most critical component is awareness of when the next action is due. Timing is determined systematically around priority. Having simple conditional formatting to create a visual cue when the due dates are getting close is essential in keeping the tool practical. This cue allows the user to prioritize their daily actions from little more than a glance.

2. **Segment**—which industry or industry segment does this opportunity sit within? For example: mining, healthcare, construction.

3. **Company Name**

4. **Location**—where is the company or project located?

5. **Contact Names**—the names of the contacts being communicated with. You don't have to know these people personally. Many of these names should be strategic. They should form the target contacts who will give access to specific customers, industries, or opportunities.

6. **Role**—this is the title, or a brief role description of the contact. You can also add their place in the stakeholder assessment, i.e., decision maker, technical expert, customer champion.

7. **Contact Details**

8. **Priority**—the priority level of the contact will define the urgency of the follow up.

9. **Action**—a historical snapshot of past actions and details of the next action required. Short summary bullet points are enough.

An example Tactical Action Plan is provided in Table 10 below.

Table 10: Example Tactical Action Plan Worksheet

Due	Seg.	Comp	Loc.	Name	Role	Contact Details	Priority	Action
29/08/22	Govt	Dept of Water	Sydney	Sarah Tomson	Project Officer	—	2	29/7/22—discussed monitoring, follow up needed 15/3/22—coffee
13/09/22	Mine	Redrock	Perth	Jenny Flair	Ops Manager	—	1	28/8/22—coffee, interested in wq meters, quote to follow by 13/9/20
25/10/22	Cons	GLD	Hillend	Basil Jet	Asset Manager	—	1	25/8/22—feedback chat, happy with service 19/4/22—regular monthly purchasing
...	...	...	...	...	...	...	...	...

This document should be considered as *living*, meaning that it evolves on a daily basis. It is a record of historical and future effort and should be easily interrogated.

The plan must incorporate a function that lets the GDBD know what actions are required in the form of a visual prompt. Otherwise, there is a strong likelihood that actions will be missed or forgotten. Adding conditional formatting—for instance, in the *due* column, color coding those actions outstanding in *red* and those approaching in *orange*—is an excellent way to keep the GDBD on point for upcoming activity. A quick glance at the tactical action plan lets you see who to contact next and in which priority order.

Systematic Priorities

Business is messy and, unfortunately, the business development function is no different. Opportunities fly in from all directions. Proposals and quotes need to be compiled and reviewed. Communications and relationships require consistent nurturing.

Keeping all these balls in the air can be impossible without some structure to keep things running. To-do lists and other techniques work for the day to day. But there needs to be a longer-term alignment of the effort, and this is what the tactical action plan is designed to assist.

The fundamental, practical component of the *triple A framework* is the systemization of the business development actions. All the effort put into the assessment and planning is boiled down to a series of systematic actions that can keep the GDBD on point with both the immediate low-hanging fruit and the strategic long-term goals.

The *prioritize* section gives some guidance on how to allocate priorities to your key customers. Go back to your list of customers now and quickly scan your three priority tiers. We now need to consider a simple framework to guide the action cadence.

How regularly do the contacts for each priority need to be actioned? Of course, this depends upon the circumstances found within your industry. As we learnt previously, existing customers should be met with regularly at first. This allows you to gain valuable feedback to help shape the future actions. This cadence can then be lengthened over time.

I define *first priority* customers as those who are in a strong position to buy. Actions should be occurring on a monthly basis so they keep your offering in the front of their minds. *Second priority* and *third priority* customers should be given a longer-term action timeframe to begin with. Once they show signs of considering your offering, the priority level and action cadence should be increased. This is summarized in the priority matrix below (Table 11).

Table 11: Example Priority Matrix

Opportunity	First Priority	Second Priority	Third Priority
Short Term	Monthly	2-Monthly	Quarterly
Long Term	2-Monthly	Quarterly	6-Monthly

This matrix allows the user to quickly consider each contact in the tactical action plan and easily allocate a due date based on the priority of the opportunity. There is a fine line between keeping your offering and brand in the mind of the customer and being perceived as annoying. Take this into account when developing your own priority matrix and adjust the timings as required.

Using the Tactical Action Plan

While execution is discussed in the next chapter, here are a few practical thoughts around using the tool.

Save Snapshots—this is a living document, and the content evolves on a daily basis. While the action column contains notes, there may be items that are deleted over time to keep the tool more manageable. Save snapshots of the document on a regular basis to make sure that any items that do fall away can be found again.

Conditional Formatting—this is perhaps the simplest yet most crucial component of turning the spreadsheet into a practical tool. Conditional formatting on the due column linked to the day's date, using color coding, creates a visual cue to make sure actions are not forgotten.

Easily Searchable—while the tactical action plan will start off small with a limited number of contacts, a proactive GDBD will grow it quickly. Therefore, making the plan easily searchable is critical. When setting up the plan, be disciplined with the consistency of your naming. This will make data interrogation that much easier and pay dividends in saved time.

Changes in the Plan—there is an old military saying, *no plan survives first contact with the enemy.* To some extent, this is true in business as well, in that, real world events will often force changes to the plan. This is when the *triple A framework* shines and can help frame your thinking and action.

For example, after meeting a key target contact, it becomes clear that they have no need for your offering at this time. That's fine—remember, *assess, aim, action.* In this instance, *assess* the opportunity again in the context of the strategic plan. *Aim* by adjusting the priority and cadence of the action. Finally, set an *action* to check in over the next six to twelve months. Or make the decision to downgrade or remove the opportunity from the list. Capture these decisions in the plan and communicate them to the larger team.

AIM Summary

In this chapter, we have focused on taking the information gathered in chapter 1 and shaping it into the three plans. This generated a series of priorities that align with the overall intent and goals of the company. However, these plans aren't built to be stuck on the wall and never looked at again. Rather, they funnel into the tactical action plan, which systematically drives the GDBD to get out and do what needs to be done. The next chapter, focusing on *action,* will look at these in more detail and give practical advice on turning action into success.

TRIPLE A: AIM—TOP TIPS

The *aim* stage of the *triple A framework* involves taking the previous assessment of your sales ecosystem and using it to plan the business development direction and effort.

—*Mine the gold that you already have*! Begin your business development efforts by focusing on your existing customers first.

—Categorizing and prioritizing your customers is vital in focusing your business development effort. Prioritize them further using the following:

—**First Priority:** Existing customers comprising the top 50 percent of your revenue or have strong growth potential.

—**Second Priority:** New customers with a strong need for your service and who are relatively easy to access with resources to afford your offering.

—**Third Priority:** Strategic customers with strong strategic value but who are harder to access.

—Always paint your customer as the *hero* and yourself as the *mentor* in your marketing messaging. Ask yourself how you can help your customer be the hero.

—A hierarchy of three plans needs to be developed to define the business development effort:

Strategic Plan: contains the overarching goals and intent of the company.

Operational Plan: covers the goals and focus areas of the business development role.

Tactical Action Plan: a daily use tool that executes on the operational plan. It identifies and prioritizes daily actions. As a living document, this plan must be regularly updated with meeting summaries and dates for further action.

TRIPLE A: AIM—FURTHER READING

—The Ansoff Matrix is very useful in figuring out which customer group to focus on first. More information can be found at http://ansoffmatrix.com/.

—*Let My People Go Surfing* by Yvon Chouinard, founder of Patagonia, is a great case study in how to add additional aligned products and customers to your portfolio. It's also a very inspirational book around company vision and purpose.

—The advantages of marketing and sales working together is explored further in Mathew Dixon and Brent Adamson's book, *The Challenger Sale: Taking Control of the Customer Conversation*.

—Donald Miller makes a very strong case for framing your customer as the hero in his book *Building a StoryBrand: Clarify Your Message So Customers Will Listen*.

—*Purple Cow: Transform Your Business by Being Remarkable* by Seth Godin is a go-to book for anyone looking to include marketing in their role.

—Simon Sinek's book *Start With Why* is essential reading if you have to develop a vision or purpose for your company as part of the strategic plan.

—Developing an action-oriented mindset is critical when building and using the tactical action plan. *Extreme Ownership: How U.S. Navy SEALs Lead and Win* by Jocko Willink and Leif Babin is essential reading here.

Business Example: AIM

Having completed a robust assessment of the ecosystem in which WCS thrives, you feel ready to move into the *aim* stage of the framework. It is time to plan the direction that your business development effort will be focused on.

You begin by taking the customer matrix and prioritizing the customers that you will start pursuing. Understanding that it is easier to *mine the gold that you already have,* you select those customers where the existing relationship is strong, and there's a history of engaging the contaminated land teams' services. This group of customers forms the *retention* segment and are prioritized first. Defining this group turns out to be pretty easy, as you already have a number of existing customer relationships who you are discussing future project opportunities with.

Knowing that the mining segment is a priority, you have identified a number of mining companies who have acquired new legacy sites with a strong likelihood of contamination issues. They will definitely need the skill set that your team provides. These companies form the *short-term acquisition* segment and are prioritized second.

Thirdly, there are a handful of very large global mining companies working from your city with many projects in operation and development. Locally, they have not been using WCS for contamination works. But the opportunity of getting a project with one of these could lead to significant future projects and a large revenue stream. Having one of these companies on the books sends a clear message to the market that you mean business. These companies form the *long-term acquisition* segment and, while important, are more strategic in nature.

You're now feeling confident in your team's place in the market, the size of the opportunities, and your target priorities. Looking back through your notes, you conduct a quick sense check of the expectations laid out by Sarah, the general manager. With relief, you realize that the expectation of $1,000,000 in revenue, while a stretch, is realistically achievable, and that you can progress full steam ahead.

Although the leadership team regularly discusses financial progress, you decide to draft your own dashboard to keep yourself and the team on point. This consists of monthly revenue and opportunity dollar targets of $83,333 and $250,000, respectively. The opportunity target has been set using the three-times revenue rule of thumb. The dashboard will form the basis of a chart to be displayed prominently above your desk, allowing the team to openly view their progress.

Systematic Planning Framework

WCS Consulting has a comprehensive business strategy that feeds effectively down to the division level. As such, there is no need to develop a new one. Instead, you simply highlight the main points from the environment division strategy and pin it to the wall. Making sure that the highlighted points are addressed, you then take all the knowledge gained so far and streamline it into an operational plan as shown below (figure 18).

WCS CONSULTING CONTAMINATED LAND TEAM OPERATIONAL PLAN

Mission

The Contaminated Land Team wants to be the go-to provider of contaminated land works across the West Australian geography in support of the wider WCS team, and our local and global tier 1 customers. The team is chasing a strong growth trajectory and is looking to grow 20% this year.

Year 1 Targets: Monthly Proposals $250,000, Monthly Revenue $83,333

Theme	Segment	Goal	Actions	KPI
Customers	Customer Experience	Market Recognition of Customer Service	Project Delivery	All projects on budget and on time
			Strong customer feedback	Quarterly feedback sought from each active customer
	Marketing	Raise Awareness of Team offering in Wider Marketplace	Implement team wide LinkedIn strategy	In place by Q1
			Present key projects to Mining Club	Scheduled by Q3
			Bring Service Line Leader to Perth to meet key strategic customer personnel	Trip scheduled for Q2
Existing Markets	Mining	Add Goal	Maintain preferred supplier status with Company A, B & C	$300,000 Revenue from Mining sector
			Develop immediate relationships with Company D, E & F	Projects gained with D, E & F by Q3
			Begin finding strategic key personnel in Company G & H	Personnel found and contacted by Q2
			Develop comprehensive capability statement	Capability statement completed by Q1
	Land Developers	Add Goal	Detail Actions	KPI for each action
Collaboration	Internal Stakeholders	Raise awareness and foster collaboration	Monthly meeting with Service Line Leader	Monthly meeting
			Monthly catch up with Infrastructure Team Leaders	Monthly meeting
			Implement Environment Division BD meeting fortnightly	Implemented by Q2
	External Stakeholders	To Add	Detail Actions	KPI for each action

Figure 18: WCS Operational Plan

The operational plan is discussed with the wider team and amended collaboratively with additional ideas. This then leads to the formation of the tactical action plan, which begins to look like the table below (Table 12):

Table 12: Example Tactical Action Plan Worksheet

Due	Seg.	Comp	Loc.	Name	Role	Contact Details	Priority	Action
14/3/22	Mining	Ariadne Resources	Perth	Andrew C	GM	—	2	14/2/22— Contact made, set up meeting to discuss CL issues
1/3/22	Mining	Bravo Mining	Perth	Paul G	Enviro Manager	—	1	15/2/22— Coffee discussion, CL issues at site 9. Needs high level proposal for desktop study
30/3/22	Land Development	Davidson Developments	Perth	Jim B	Project Director	—	1	30/1/22— No immediate projects, Carl to touch base in two months to check in
. . .	. . .	. . .	. . .	. . .	. . .	. . .	. . .	. . .

Your initial tactical action plan comprises fifty preliminary entries, each with a due date and action. Internal and external stakeholders are also included to ensure they are contacted regularly. It is intended that more customer targets be added over time.

To make the business development a shared effort within the team, you add an additional column titled *responsible* and assign some of your team to follow up. The tool now forms the living backbone of the business development effort for the entire contaminated land sites team. While you ultimately have accountability for the business development, sharing it with the rest of the team allows everyone to share upcoming action outcomes and market intelligence.

WCS AIM Summary

Your team now has the three plans for the contaminated land service, detailing the business development effort, direction, and shared responsibility. The tactical action plan will act as an evolving, living document, systematically flagging customer and stakeholder action so that nothing gets missed. Now you are ready to start contacting customers and bringing in more work.

TRIPLE A: ACTION

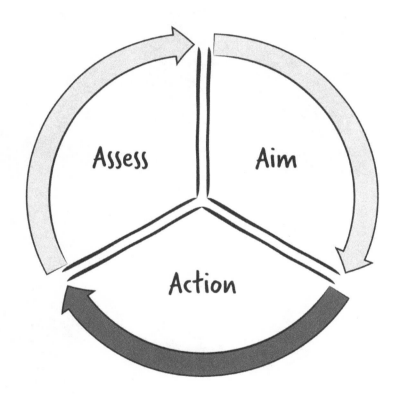

We are now looking at the third, and arguably the most important, *A* in the *triple A framework—action*. This is really the systematic execution of all the work and planning developed in the previous chapters.

It is easy to get caught up with enthusiasm after the *assess* and *aim* stages of the *triple A framework* and put a lot of energy in chasing and meeting the priority targets. Where the GDBD really shines is after that initial wave of enthusiasm has worn off. They still chase the opportunities, still make the calls, and still seek feedback from customers and stakeholders. And all this is done in line with the intent and actions incorporated in the three plans.

But how do you stay on target?

The secret is *systematic* action implementation. Using the tactical action plan will prompt and guide regular activity in line with the outcomes desired by the organization and team. This chapter will provide practical implementation advice on turning the *assess* and *aim* stages into tangible sales outcomes.

Measuring Your Success

The first thing to consider before implementation is the systematic measurement of results. One of the key attributes of the GDBD is measuring success. You must monitor the success of your efforts and have a handle on the opportunities entering the top of the funnel and the revenue falling out the bottom. If numbers drop, the GDBD must be aware immediately. Leading and lagging indicators are vital here.

A leading indicator is one that forecasts the future-expected revenue and highlights the effort being placed into filling the sales funnel. There are many different metrics that can be measured, including number of meetings, calls, quotes, created leads/opportunities, new accounts, and won opportunities.

Tracking and reporting the numbers on all of these produces too much work. I have found that the simplest and easiest leading indicator to track is the dollar value of the opportunities issued that month. This wraps all the activity into an easily translatable number. If the GDBD is implementing the plan successfully, the opportunity value should be high. If the opportunity value is low, questions need to be asked to understand why.

What should the opportunity value be compared against? Of course, each industry is different, but a useful rule of thumb that has treated me well over the years is three times your monthly sales budget. If you know the market and have an offering that is appealing, a three-times quoting value should yield the results you need. Of course, looking at past opportunities and revenue will provide a good indication of the rate that can be extrapolated to a target opportunity value.

A lagging indicator is one that shows how successful you have been and is firmly planted in past performance. These include won and lost opportunities and won and lost revenue. Again, there is a real danger in monitoring and analyzing too many variables here.

For a simple trend that shows how the business development is performing, track revenue month by month.

The revenue can be split further if more detail is required. It is my opinion, however, that this has the tendency to devour time that could be better spent developing relationships and pursuing opportunities. Use the KISS principal—*keep it simple, stupid*—to make the graphs easy to understand.

An example graph is presented in figure 19. As you can see, this is uncluttered and easy to interpret. It displays the following:

- **Monthly Sales**—revenue made that month, *lagging indicator*.
- **Monthly Quotes**—total dollar value of opportunities this month, *leading indicator* giving a signal of future revenue success.
- **YTD Sales**—cumulative monthly revenue allowing progress against the year's sales budget.
- **YTD Budget**—cumulative month-by-month sales targets by which your revenue is measured.

This snapshot can act as a simple dashboard to show the health of the business development function. These trends then prompt further interrogation as required. For example, a dip in quoting would require justification and redemptive action, while a spike in revenue would require an explanation on what worked well. A GDBD must know how they are performing and understand the story behind the numbers they are tracking.

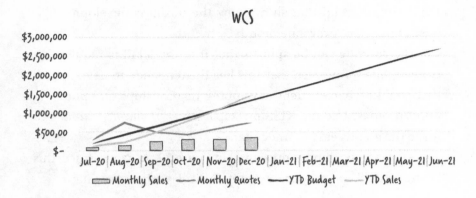

Figure 19: Example performance tracking graph

Methodical Marketing

Looking back at the sales funnel figure from a previous chapter, the first stage in creating opportunities is filling the funnel with leads. A key component of keeping it full is through systematic marketing. Website development and SEO are important and take a very special skill set, which is outside the remit of this book, and I will assume it is outsourced to either the marketing department or an external provider. Where the GDBD can have real impact and complete control of their activity is in social media, and in particular, LinkedIn.

Although LinkedIn originally began as a tool for recruiters, it has firmly established itself as the social platform for business. As such, it lends itself as the perfect tool to initiate business-to-business marketing—marketing, *not* selling. This cannot be emphasized enough. The platform is there to grow and nurture a network of business connections, and the quickest way to lose these connections is to directly sell to them.

Utilizing LinkedIn systematically, day to day, is an excellent way to generate brand awareness, developing leads and positions for both the brand and the GDBD. Taking ten minutes a day on the platform and spending an hour crafting two posts a week can begin to generate results relatively quickly.

There are many courses and experts pushing their LinkedIn expertise and charging a lot of money for the privilege. However, getting started is not that difficult. Below, I highlight a simple daily system that you can follow. It draws upon the *assess* and *aim* stages of the *triple A framework*, which you have already developed.

Five-Minute LinkedIn Marketing

Before we start developing your LinkedIn system, we need to consider what the aim of the campaign is going to be. The overall objective should be: *provide a steady source of leads to the top of the sales funnel.*

This translates as the marketing effort adding opportunities and revenue into your sales pathway. The specific mission that supports the objective can be broken down into three tasks:

1. Position the GDBD and company as experts within their niche.
2. Generate regular touch points for the company brand, building recognition over time.
3. Develop a network of connections who are interested in your company offering.

The actions required to achieve the mission tasks can be divided into 3 Ps:

- **Profile**—create a great first impression for yourself and your company.
- **Propagate**—develop a network of connections who are interested in your offering.

- **Promote**—generate touch points and value-based content to produce interest, brand awareness, and trust in your offering.

Profile

If you have a quick scan through the LinkedIn profiles of your connections, it is obvious that most people have structured their profiles like an online resume. This makes sense since LinkedIn was originally designed as a tool for recruiters. However, the profile of a GDBD should focus on what they are offering to the market.

Think of your profile as your customers' first impression of your company and the opportunity to highlight the unique aspects about what your offering comprises. When redesigning your profile, use the following four points to guide you.

Stand out and be compelling. Highlight your company offering in your headline and make sure your photograph conveys professionalism.

Add detail around your company offering. A quick scan of your profile should let the reader understand the key ways that you can help them.

Use key words throughout your profile. Think of these as words that potential customers would type into Google if they were looking for your offering. For example, if your niche was flood modeling, you would include words and phrases like, flood modeling, flooding, flood specialist, flood mapping etc. Make sure these are mentioned a number of times throughout your profile.

Make it easy for the connection. The aim of using LinkedIn is to get a steady stream of leads entering the sales funnel, so make it easy for interested connections to learn more. Put your contact details in the *about* section, your company phone number and email address, and add a link to the relevant pages of your company website.

Propagate

Now that the profile really highlights what your offering is and provides an easy way to engage with you, it is time to start making connections. There are three degrees of connection as shown in figure 20.

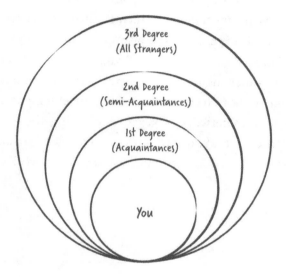

Figure 20: Degrees of connection in LinkedIn

These are described as follows:

1. First-degree connection—contacts that have connected to you. You want to either know these people directly or have something in common. Preferably industry and geography.
2. Second-degree connection—contacts who are connected to your first-degree connections. Generally, you don't know these people, though you will have acquaintances in common.
3. Third-degree connection—contacts outside of your immediate network. To connect with them, you will need to broaden the reach of your second-degree connections.

Not all connections are equal. Do not fall into the trap of connecting to everyone. This is completely counterproductive and will significantly dilute your efforts. Connections need to be hyper-focused on individuals who are relevant, who may have an interest in, or a need for, your offering.

Revisit the work done on your ideal customer and look at the key customers in your operational plan. Which roles within the key customers have the most interest and influence around your company offering? Once this is established, a simple search will yield gold. For example, principal water engineer, Sydney, would generate a list of principal level water engineers in the Sydney area. I have found that the more specific the search criteria is, the more useful the results will be.

Building your network is key to leveraging the power of the LinkedIn platform. Make a commitment to connect to thirty relevant second-degree connections every day, and your network will expand dramatically.

Promote

When people connect to you and view your profile, that is one touch point for your brand. Developing your burgeoning network and providing further touch points around your brand is an efficient way to begin sourcing leads. You can do this in two simple ways by:

- **Responding to accepted connections**
- **Posting value-add material**

If someone accepts your invitation to connect, it indicates that they have some interest in what you have to offer. Developing a simple conversation script that generates further touch points is a quick method to uncovering leads. A simple script might look like the following:

Company: Hi, thanks for connecting. Regards, Chris.

Customer response: No problem. My pleasure.

Company: How are you finding the market at the moment? Keeping busy?

Customer: Pretty busy at the moment.

Company: We're pretty steady at the moment too. How do you manage your contaminated land issues?

Customer response: We manage it well at the moment but could do with some extra field staff.

Company: If you need any advice on contaminated land investigations, feel free to give me a call.

Keeping the messages short and to the point often incites a reply. No one wants to read long or boring messages on the platform. While tailoring your response to the lead's reactions is important, a simple script like this can maintain consistent messaging and significantly speed up interaction times.

Regular posting on LinkedIn for your target audience is another simple way to keep your company offering front of mind. These posts should not be focused on sales but rather focused on adding value through teaching, providing new information, or looking at things from a different perspective. Use this opportunity to cement your position as a specialist within the industry or niche.

Relevant posts centered on your offering form valuable touch points that get your customer base thinking about what you do and not what you sell. This is a small but significant difference in gaining the trust of the buyer. Consistently posting twice a week is enough to start gaining traction and leads. Don't forget that results won't happen overnight, and consistent action is a must to achieving growth.

If you are not sure how to message your offering appropriately, I'll repeat my advice from the chapter on five-minute marketing.

Read Donald Miller's book, *Building a StoryBrand*, and frame your customer as the hero.

Being consistent in adding connections and posting within LinkedIn will yield leads. It is crucial that when someone shows interest in your offering, you respond fast. Make sure to take the conversation off LinkedIn as quickly as possible. Transfer to email first and face-to-face once the lead is qualified as an opportunity.

Systematic Sales Path

As discussed in the previous chapter, the tactical action plan should be used to systematically drive business development activity. While this tool is a critical part of the process, it forms part of the systematic sales path. This comprises the flow of actions that take place once an opportunity has been recognized. In his book, *Business Made Simple*, Donald Miller summarizes a simple sales path as the following steps:

1. Qualify the lead.
2. Send the lead information and schedule a call.
3. Engage in an intake meeting.
4. Send the proposal.
5. Enter the closing sequence.

This path forms a good baseline, but I want to get a bit more specific around the stages of the process and what a GDBD should be doing. I also believe that the business development path actually extends up the sales funnel into lead generation, and that this part of the funnel should also be systemized.

The systematic sales path follows the stages of the sales funnel and comprises three sections (figure 21). The first, *development*, is directed by the tactical action plan and comprises a cycle of activities around the development of relationships within the target customer base. This works concurrently with the other marketing efforts to generate and develop leads.

The second part of the systematic sales path is *lead qualification*, sandwiched between the *development* and *pursuit* stages. This provides an efficient way to qualify whether a lead can be considered a real opportunity for the business and whether time and effort should be spent in pursuit. A robust qualification process tailored to the individual company makes sure that the GDBD's effort is spent on real opportunities with potential to yield revenue.

The third stage, *pursuit*, contains the series of actions to follow once you have identified a qualified lead. Each action is designed to enable the GDBD to engage with the customer, learn what it is that they really need, and respond appropriately.

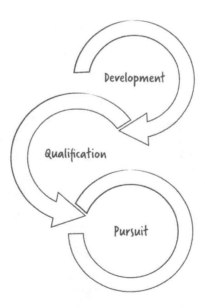

Figure 21: Systematic Sales Path

The stages of the systematic sales path are there to act as a guide; they should be understood, then adapted to your own unique set of industry circumstances.

One point to bear in mind is that the sales process for your business should be the same regardless of the sales cycle time. If your business has long and short sales cycles, the same process should be followed for both. This ensures consistency in the way customers are treated while making sure that all sales are given the strongest chance to succeed.

Systematic Development

Systematic development is the nurturing of relationships with key personnel from the target organizations identified in the tactical action plan. Below is a sequence of actions that can be undertaken to begin developing these contacts. The systematic development phase is illustrated in figure 22.

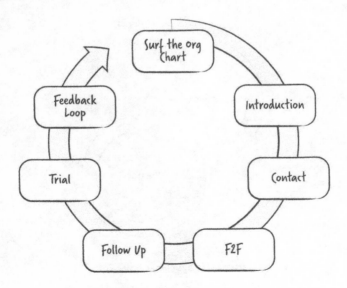

Figure 22: Systematic Development Phase

1. Surf the Org Chart

This term was coined by one of my mentors, Greg Hardwich (2019). It really encapsulates the concept of identifying a who's who of the stakeholders and decision makers within your target customer organizations. Getting hold of a customer organizational chart can be virtually impossible. LinkedIn is the ideal tool to identify a few key personnel to follow up with. Ideally, these are customers with a use for your company offering or leading the teams who would be using it.

You must connect with different levels within the customer organization—leaders, frontline workers, and budget holders. Having multiple levels aware of your offering makes their decision to buy that much easier. If the frontline workers request your services and the leaders and budget holders already understand the value, the funds are much easier to release.

Don't fall into the trap of having only a single contact within a customer organization. Once that contact leaves, the relationship vanishes. It becomes all too easy for that customer to seek your offering elsewhere.

2. Introduction

For existing customers, the introduction is pretty straightforward. Asking for a meeting to gain feedback on your company's performance to date allows you to meet with a clear agenda that doesn't feel salesy. Remember to listen to the feedback they provide and take notes for later.

Gaining a meaningful introduction to a new potential customer can be the hardest part of the entire process. How do you get them to talk to you, let alone to meet you in person? The answer is *don't be a salesperson.*

What I mean by that is put yourself in their shoes. Their time is precious—why should they spend it in discussion with you? Make sure that what you have to offer is relevant to them.

Have a deep understanding of your customer's problem and how you can help them solve it.

One of the best ways to get an introduction is to get a referral from a mutual acquaintance who believes there is value in you meeting. Talk to your personal network and existing customers to see if they can help you get an introduction.

3. Contact

Once an introduction is secured, make contact via email or phone. The latter is more personable. With emails, be careful that your tone doesn't come over as spam-like. This isn't the time for a hard sell. Keep phone calls and emails short and to the point. Brevity is key. Just say who you are, who recommended you meet, and what you want to discuss.

If they say no, don't feel despondent. Perhaps they're not yet ready for your services. Always be polite and professional; you may well be dealing with them in the future. Make a note on the tactical action plan and move on to the next one, remembering to place a date to loop back to that contact again in the future.

4. Face-to-Face

Now the contact has agreed to meet. Don't be nervous— they are meeting because of an interest in the agenda from your previous communication. Make sure that you stick to that agenda. You don't want your customer to feel ambushed. Ask questions and listen to the answers. Do not spend all your time talking about how great your offering and company are. Use the 80:20 rule, 80 percent listening and 20 percent talking.

Learn as much as you can from the contact. Tell them a little about what your company does and how you believe it can help in relation to what you've heard them say. Be polite and ask permission to reach out to them again in the future.

5. Follow up

Once the meeting is complete, make sure to follow up fast. A quick email thanking them for their time and providing any information they may have asked for is enough. Adjust the tactical action plan with relevant notes, and set a date for a follow-up based on priority and opportunity potential.

6. Trial

Having learned from the meeting about where the customer needs help, consider a way to let them experience your offering with little risk or expense. Perhaps you could invite them to your factory for a tour or provide some free training.

Alternatively, provide them with existing customers who are willing to act as a reference. Allowing the customer to experience what you have to offer can help develop their sense of trust in your company and offering, which can go a long way in reducing any concerns they may have of taking a risk on a new company.

If the customer has discussed a specific problem that you can solve, don't just send a quote, prepare a proposal. Include the costs. But you also need to reassure the customer that you understand their problem; explain how you can solve it. Make sure to highlight what the benefits will be once your solution is engaged. The proposal can take the form of a letter, formal document, or email. This will very much depend on the customer's expectations. Regardless, placing your offering into context is key.

7. Feedback Loop

In addition to updating the tactical action plan, it is critical that the information learned in the meeting is fed back into the wider business. Taking time to share findings during the leadership or team meetings is important so the organization can adapt. Don't forget to include your internal stakeholders and influencers as part of this communication. The adaptive feedback loop will be discussed later in this book.

Lead Qualification

The second phase of the systematic sales path is *lead qualification*. This involves a fast assessment of leads to determine their worth as an opportunity. It is an integral part of the whole sales process. But it shouldn't be onerous.

When I worked in a large national engineering company, we had a very robust qualification process that consisted of a GO/NO-GO meeting (this company had an excellent GO/NO-GO form, which I have used as a basis for the qualification checklist below). The meeting comprised at least four high-level personnel, plus the bid/project manager. By the time a decision had been reached, a large amount of money had already been spent. This is fine if you are pursuing $100,000+ opportunities, but on smaller prospects, the profit had been burned from the project before it has even been quoted.

Donald Miller's Business Made Simple company has a whole team dedicated to qualifying leads as they come in. This allows their sales team to focus on the selling of their products, geared toward customers who are actually interested (Miller 2021).

In this instance, we are assuming that the GDBD is either alone or part of a small team, and that a dedicated team of lead qualifiers is, unfortunately, not part of the picture. The qualification process should be fast, intuitive, and easy to use. Below is a quick series of questions that can form a qualification checklist (figure 23). Adapt this to your own set of circumstances.

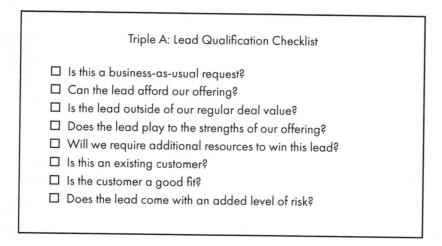

Figure 23: Lead Qualification Checklist

The answers to these questions should provide clear guidance as to whether you should qualify the lead and progress it to the systematic *pursuit* stage. Each of the questions should have an action/response associated with it. Let's look at each question in more detail.

1. Is this a business-as-usual request?
   Is the lead related to business-as-usual activities? If yes, change the lead to an opportunity and pursue. If no, can we deliver on the opportunity?

2. Can the lead afford our offering?
   If no, disqualify the lead.

3. Is the lead outside our regular deal value?
   If the dollar value is much larger than normal, proceed only after further discussions with the wider team to make sure an opportunity of that size can be delivered.

4. Does the lead play to the strengths of our offering?
    If the lead does align with the offering strengths, then change
    to an opportunity. If it does not, then additional assessment
    will be required around whether it aligns with the other parts
    of the operational plan.

5. Will we require additional resources to win this lead?
    If yes, do we have those resources available? If no, then do not
    qualify. A half-baked proposal can do significant damage to
    the company's reputation. It is better to send nothing at all
    than to send something substandard.

6. Is this an existing customer?
    Remember the Ansoff Matrix in the *assess* chapter? It's
    always better to sell to existing customers who already know
    your offering and can be more supportive if you are trying
    something new.

7. Is the customer a good fit?
    Does the customer fit within the preferred customer profile?
    If yes, qualify. If no, do not qualify.

8. Does the opportunity come with an added level of risk?
    Consider, for example, any reputational, financial, or safety
    risks associated with the opportunity. Risks can take many
    forms and need to be considered carefully. If high risk looks
    likely, a discussion with the leadership team should be
    initiated and the risks mitigated if the lead is to be qualified.

The qualification checklist will be different for each company,
and you should consider what is important for your particular
circumstances and adjust accordingly. It is even possible to incorporate
the company values into the qualification checklist. I've seen this done

really well with a question like, *Is the opportunity based within the tobacco, whaling, or nuclear industry? If yes, do not qualify.*

This is a clear message to the business development function that this organization does not support projects within those industries. Are there any nonnegotiables that you can incorporate into your own version?

Systematic Pursuit

Sam, a good friend of mine, had spent months perfecting his side hustle handcrafting beautiful wooden furniture. He had identified a niche customer in the creative corporate space who valued fine craftsmanship, sustainable materials, and local business. Feeling inspired, he set up his digital marketing, which lead to him having a couple of face-to-face meetings. From there, a number of leads rolled in that qualified as opportunities.

Everything seemed suddenly real. The side hustle had the potential to sell. Sam froze, afraid of taking the next step. He procrastinated, and opportunities with the potential to make significant revenue sat there doing nothing.

Sam explained his dilemma to me over a beer, and I laid out a simple systematic pursuit process, on the back of a paper napkin, focused on the key points—clarify, call, meet, send proposal, follow up, and adjust. As I was sharing this process, I could sense Sam's demeanor changing from subdued to excited over the span of ten minutes. I got a call a week later to let me know that he had secured his first sale.

Opportunities are an indication that the customer has identified a need for your company offering and wants to learn more. These must be actioned, and the customer must be engaged with as quickly as possible. Ask yourself this—would you rather buy from a company that sends you a price via email, or a company that calls and takes the time to understand what you are looking for?

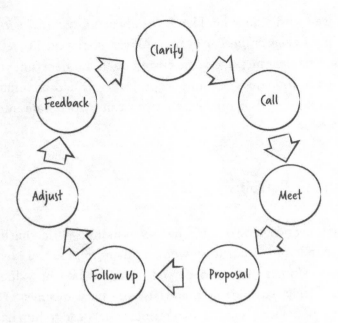

Figure 24: Systematic Pursuit

Once a lead has qualified as an opportunity, what happens next? It is crucial that you run all opportunities through the same process so that nothing is missed and that they are all dealt with consistently. This is where the systematic pursuit process comes in. Below, I've detailed a simple systematic pursuit process, based on the scribbles I'd developed for Sam back in the day. Systematically leading your customers through this process vastly improves your chances of turning those opportunities into revenue. The systematic pursuit is illustrated in figure 24.

1. **Clarify**—carefully examine what the customer is asking for and define a list of questions that need clarification. This shows the customer that you know your subject and are interested in finding them the right solution.

2. **Call**—a qualified lead means that someone is curious about your company offering and wants to learn more. I cannot emphasize this enough—pick up the phone and call them. Ask clarification questions and listen to the answers. Make sure to get answers to all the items determined in stage one. Putting a human face (or voice) to the organization will set you apart from the majority of your customers.

3. **Meet**—if the opportunity is particularly large or complex, arrange a face-to-face meeting where points can be clarified, concerns discussed, and where a deeper dive can be provided on solving your customer's problem. Again, ask questions and listen. You need to be the customer's guide, not the hero trying to showcase how great your company is.

4. **Proposal**—simply sending a quote with a price is not enough. There needs to be context around what you are offering and how it is going to assist the customer in their specific situation. It does not need to be complicated or lengthy; in fact, brevity is preferred. The customer needs to be able to skim the document and know why they should be using your offering. A simple explanation with key bullet points should be enough for most proposals.

5. **Follow Up**—this critical stage is often forgotten, as even seasoned business developers will sometimes immediately move on to the next opportunity following submission of a proposal. Give the customer time to read the proposal, and then follow up with a call. Does it meet the requirements? Is the price point right? Get valuable feedback—without it, you can't adjust your offer.

6. **Adjust**—once you have the proposal feedback from the customer, don't waste it. If possible, adjust your offer based on the customer conversation and resubmit a version that is more aligned to the customer expectations.

7. **Feedback Request**—once the opportunity has been won or lost, use this as a way to open up further dialogue with the customer. Ask for feedback on why the proposal was won or lost and be sure to listen. Use this to sense check your assumptions and loop into the *assess* and *aim* stages of the *triple A framework*. Discuss this feedback with the leadership team, as there may be gold in adapting the organization for future wins.

Customer Meetings

I often get asked how to act when meeting customers, both existing and prospective. Having been on both sides of the business development conversation, I have seen good and bad examples.

Picture this—a business development manager from a large tracking software company reached out to me via LinkedIn and asked to meet. The product he was selling would add benefit to the role I was in, so I was interested in learning more. He suggested meeting in a coffee shop near where I was working.

First, he was ten minutes late, not a good start. Second, he didn't offer to buy me a coffee; instead, he launched directly into his pitch. I had to stop him and go and buy my own coffee, politely offering to get him one also. To be honest, his product could have held the answers to all my project tracking needs, but I was no longer interested in listening to what he had to say; I drank my coffee as fast as I could before closing the meeting down.

A better example was a business coach who I met through a

board I was serving on. We grabbed a coffee, and he asked me about my leadership journey and any issues I was facing. After he learned about the problems I was tackling, he proceeded to explain how he would guide me through these challenges and what success might look like. I left the meeting feeling that I had learned something and, importantly, that I wanted to learn more. Needless to say, I became Greg's customer for many years.

Stephen Covey's *Habit 5: Seek First to Understand, Then to Be Understood* could not be more aligned to my message. Listen to your customer. Ask pertinent questions and understand the context around their issue. Only once you've understood them can you begin to start solving their problems.

Donald Millers' *StoryBrand* really encapsulates the idea that a company should act as a guide to their customers, helping them to become the hero. By extension, the GDBD should be the physical representation of that guide, leading the customer on the hero's journey. Ask pertinent questions, listen, and advise. Don't talk about yourself and how great your company is. Make the customer the center of the conversation and react to that.

Updating the tactical action plan after each customer meeting is essential. Add a brief one-line summary to the *action* column with enough information to trigger the memory. Update the date for the next meeting in line with the predetermined priority cadence developed previously or based on the needs of the opportunity. Any immediate actions should be moved on to your daily task list. Finally, any interesting information about the state of the market or customer direction should be noted and passed on to the wider team.

Proposal

If the customer meeting goes well, you may be offered a chance to quote for the provision of a piece of work or a product. This is more than just a formality. Sales can be won and lost on the proposal and should reiterate and enhance the previous discussions. Some quotes are small enough that an accompanying email covering some key selling points is enough. But for larger or more complicated opportunities, a proposal is critical.

The triple A proposal framework comprises:

1. **Introduction**—include a thanks for the opportunity and a three-point summary of the unique aspects of the proposal.

2. **Problem**—outline the problem you have been asked to solve. Make sure to accurately define the scope of work here. Align expectations between yourself and the customer.

3. **Product/Service**—explain what your product or service comprises and how it will solve the customer's problem.

4. **Plan**—describe your execution plan, including timeframes.

5. **Price and Options**—detail the pricing structure of your offering.

6. **Resolution**—what will the end result, or solved problem, look like for the customer?

Broken down like this, a proposal is not a complicated document to produce. Developing a template that encapsulates the six points, which can be quickly edited in line with customer expectations, can be a real timesaver that easily maintains the consistency of your sales messaging.

Follow Up

When sending a proposal to a customer, make sure that you follow up with a call within a week. This gives the customer enough time to read your proposal and digest the content. Make good on your promise and follow up with a phone call to discuss the contents. Ask for further clarification on the following:

- Is it what you are looking for?
- Does the scope cover everything required?
- How is the price point?
- Is there anything missing?

Use this as an opportunity to tweak your offering to align with the customer expectations. At the end of the discussion, if the customer feedback has raised any issues, ask their permission to amend the proposal and resubmit it. This will give you one more opportunity to give the customer exactly what they are looking for—one more opportunity to win the sale.

It must be noted that some customers, in particular government departments, will not allow follow-up discussions. In this instance, accept this as the case and move on to the next action on your tactical action plan.

Tracking Large Opportunities

During the business development cycle, certain opportunities will present themselves that are particularly large or strategic in nature. Perhaps there is potential for a significant recurring order or a first project with a key customer target. It is important to track these key opportunities separately to the regular flow filtering through your sales funnel. Their importance merits additional effort. I refer to these as *must-win* opportunities, which really highlights their significance to the objectives of the organization. Each company defines *must-win* in a different way, but the classification could include:

- **High revenue potential**
- **Long-term revenue potential**
- **New strategic customer onboarding**
- **Industry reputation enhancement**
- **New service/product showcase opportunity**

I'm a very visual person and find it useful to be able to see how these larger opportunities are progressing. Greg Hardwich developed an excellent tool called the *opportunity qualification matrix*, which I have simplified for our purposes.

To start, create the following matrix (figure 25). This can be made digitally, though my preference is to draw it on a large whiteboard.

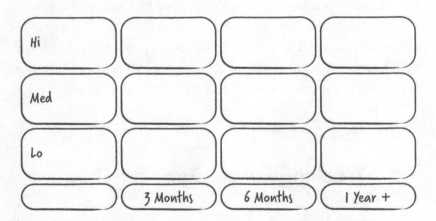

Figure 25: Must-Win Opportunity Matrix (based on initial work by Hardwich)

This simple matrix comprises *timeframe* on the horizontal, which represents the time in which the opportunity will be awarded by the client. The length of your sales cycle will determine the timeframes used, though typically the *must-wins* are those with a longer sales cycle than your regular opportunities.

The vertical axis represents the likelihood of winning the opportunity and is divided into three stages of probability. The definition of these will depend on your particular circumstances, but as a guide, I use:

- High
  —Engaged; strong customer relationship.
  —Detailed project discussions and aligned proposal submitted.

- Med
  —Discussion. Good customer relationship.
  —Limited project discussions; proposal likely to be requested.

- Low
  —Awareness; little to no customer relationship.
  —No discussions to date; proposal unlikely to be requested at this time.

The probability axis definitions should be stated in a way that makes it easy to move an opportunity as it progresses through the sales cycle.

To populate this matrix with your *must-wins* means making sure that the body of the matrix is large enough to house them. Mine sits on the wall on a one-meter board, and while it is nothing fancy, it allows me to easily move the *must-wins* from square to square as new information comes to light.

Next, the matrix must be populated with the opportunities themselves. These should have just enough information so that the user can quickly discern what they are. As an example, I use Post-it notes with the following information:

- **Project Name**
- **Customer Name**
- **Product/Service Required**
- **Likely Date of Award**

This is enough information to allow cross-reference with the tactical action plan, where specific actions with key personnel and stakeholders should be placed.

Once the information is on the Post-it notes, or digital sticky note, it is time to place it on the matrix. Check the timeframe and likelihood of winning, and place the opportunity within the correct square (figure 26). The matrix needs to be user-friendly, so don't overpopulate or create a lost sea of notes. Only include those that are of most significance to the business.

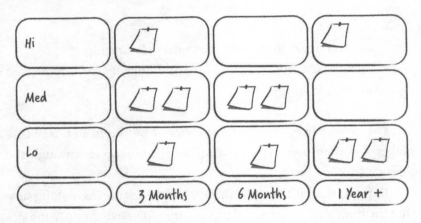

Figure 26: Populated Must-Win Opportunity Matrix

Having long-term visibility of opportunities is crucial for your strategic success. To really work, the visibility needs to be converted into action. The goal of the matrix is to be able to move *must-wins* from a *low* to a *high* likelihood of success (figure 27). A quick look at the matrix highlights which companies to talk to about which projects, and these actions should be placed into the tactical action plan under high priority and with appropriate due dates.

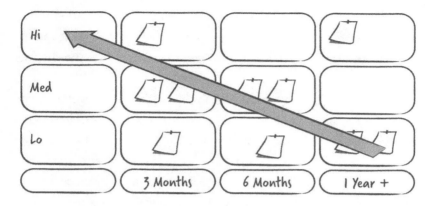

Figure 27: Goal of the Must-Win Matrix

Much like the tactical action plan, the matrix must be *living*, which means it needs to be regularly and accurately updated to reflect the real-world situation. Opportunities should be moved as soon as information gleaned from customers and stakeholders is heard.

Good practice involves taking fifteen minutes a week to survey the matrix with the team and discuss any new information, make changes to the matrix, and allocate actions to the tactical action plan. Having others involved can draw out additional information and insight that the individual GDBD may miss on their own.

Maintaining Purpose (Adaptive Feedback Loop)

Think back to the sales ecosystem discussed at the beginning of this book. The GDBD forms a critical conduit of information flowing into and out of the organization. The GDBD is out in the market talking to customers and working with them to understand their perspectives. They are talking to project teams and other stakeholders and tracking future projects.

Ultimately, the GDBD becomes the hub of customer and market information and, by extension, is the company expert on these things. No other person in your organization is as qualified to be the channel for this information.

Of course, collecting the market information and using it to create actions in the tactical action plan is essential, but the real gold is when this information is fed back into the wider organization. It needs to be heard by the leadership team, where it can be acted on if necessary. Changes in customer behavior need to be understood by those making the strategic decisions, and the GDBD should be the source of that information. I mentioned right at the beginning of the book that the business development function must have a seat at the leadership table, otherwise the impact and regularity of market feedback will be lost.

The adaptive feedback loop works best when valuable information is passed to the strategic decision makers who can adapt company practice in response. This is vital in maintaining company flexibility in a world where markets are disrupted with alarming regularity. In the following section, we will explore the *what*, *who*, and *where* of the adaptive feedback loop so that you can start using it in your own role.

The *What* of Feedback

A GDBD is out in the market every day, gleaning reams of information and adjusting the must-win matrix and tactical action plan. Project, customer, and competitor information is everywhere. For people to listen, you need to discern what you share. It needs to be relevant and strategic in nature.

Strategic information is not whether Company X is buying thirty widgets, but rather, what the larger trends with bigger implications are. For example, why is Company X buying the widgets, and how might it affect your organization? The information to consider feeding back includes the following:

Customer Feedback—this is crucial to understand how your offering is being perceived, the good and the bad. Particularly important are any trends in the feedback. Has there been a string of complaints around a certain offering, or has one of the project teams been getting praised by numerous clients?

Market Trends—are there any trends in the market that are being identified by the customer and industry stakeholders? How are these likely to impact future sales and customer buying behaviors?

Customer Trends—are there any significant trends regarding specific customers? Is an upcoming merger or restructure likely to change their buying behavior, and what will the potential impact be?

Competitor News—what are your major competitors doing? Who are they targeting, and what is their pricing strategy? Are they displaying competitive behavior, and what might this mean for your business? Have they changed how they do things?

Opportunity News—what are the large opportunities that are sitting over the horizon, and what action is needed to position your team for a future win?

This information goes beyond the regular day-to-day sales transactions and instead looks at the sales ecosystem through a strategic lens. It is vital that this data is disseminated to the wider team so that, collectively, the company can adapt as required.

The *Who* of Feedback

We have established the importance of the GDBD feeding information from the wider market and industry back into the company to allow adaptive change to occur. But who needs to get this information? The "Internal Stakeholder" section provides a list of relevant personnel in addition to the leadership team and the product managers in charge of altering the company offering.

Be aware that each will be interested in slightly different

information. Remember, if you are not sure what information they want to hear, ask. Summary points around some of the stakeholders you may need to provide market insights to are presented below:

Leadership Team—setting the strategic direction of the company is typically controlled either by the owner, the managing director, or the executive management. In smaller companies, access to these personnel is fairly straightforward. The larger the company, the more levels of management appear.

As a business developer for a business unit or division, you should adhere to the chain of command and feedback the information to the divisional leadership team. They will want to know the strategic information and trends that will be impacting the organization over the long term. Revenue and pricing trends and the impact on the bottom line are crucial to this group, as they are usually measured on these numbers.

Product Manager—this individual is in charge of a particular product or service line and has influence on the delivery. Customer trends are critical to this person, as they will need to adjust the product offering in line with what the customers are looking for.

Research and Development Team—similar to the product manager, the research and development team are looking to produce new company offerings over the long term. They need the long-term market and customer trends, particularly in light of the new market and product sections of the Ansoff Matrix. Information gained from the GDBD can shape the future products and services of the company.

Subject Matter Experts—the experts should be aware of market trends. But it can be very useful to discuss these with them. Getting their perspective may open up your understanding of events and trends.

Team Leaders—these staff members are running the teams who are delivering the company offering to the customer base. They need to know the shorter-term trends, particularly around the customer and upcoming opportunities. This can add real depth to their customer interactions and allow them to plan team resourcing.

Marketing Team—the marketing team is responsible for pushing the company offering out to the market. Short-, medium-, and long-term market trends are critical to their campaign planning. Any customer feedback on the company offering—and specifically around the customer reaction to marketing campaigns—will be appreciated.

It should be obvious by now that the information gained by a GDBD is critical to the decision-making at all levels of the business. It is, therefore, your duty to disseminate this information regularly and widely so that it can help inform and shape the future health of your organization.

The *Where* of Feedback

As a GDBD, you have access to a vast wealth of time-sensitive information, and you are aware of who you should be sharing it with. But what is the best way to get this information to the right people in a timely manner? In my opinion, there needs to be time allocated in the division or company leadership meetings where the GDBD can summarize their findings for that week. This only needs a broad synopsis, with deeper dives into the information being taken separately from the meeting.

Make the time to share this information with interested personnel through quick, scheduled, or informal catch ups, which should then be captured in the tactical action plan. It is important to not let these meetings become a time sink; remember that most of your time needs to be out in the market with the customers.

While regular feedback is important, market and customer intelligence must form part of the strategic and operational planning. Discuss this with your leadership team and find the best way to impart this knowledge into the process. Perhaps this could take the form of an evidence-based presentation or report. Better yet, it could be a seat at the table during strategy formation and assessment. Bear in mind that this seat needs to be earned through your gained knowledge and understanding of what's happening in the market. To gain that information takes implementation of the systematic sales process detailed throughout this book.

ACTION Summary

Having finished the *action* chapter, you are armed to begin executing the systematic sales path—getting out into the market, talking to customers, pursuing opportunities, and feeding back to your organization. All this activity is aligned with your findings and planned intent from the *assess* and *aim* chapters. Being systematic allows opportunities to progress down the sales path with consistency, preventing them from being forgotten in the scrum of day-to-day priorities.

In addition to winning opportunities and boosting the revenue of your organization, the GDBD is the main conduit between the market and the company. Make use of this unique position; discuss market and customer information with the relevant stakeholders within your enterprise.

Consistency in your work ethic, delivering a systematic approach to customer relationships, and proactively developing opportunities will cement your position as a professional, results-driven business developer—an invaluable member of the team.

TRIPLE A: ACTION—TOP TIPS

The *action* stage of the *triple A framework* dovetails all the work from *assess* and *aim* into daily result-focused activity. It comprises an ongoing systematic process for contacting customers and encouraging them to utilize your company offering.

—To be successful, you must measure progress. A simple way to do this is through volume of quotes/opportunities (*leading indicator*) and volume of revenue (*lagging indicator*). Tracking both gives a useful snapshot of growth.

—LinkedIn is an excellent and free marketing resource. Use it.

—The systematic sales path consists of *development, qualification,* and *pursuit.*

—**Systematic Development:** nurturing of relationships with key personnel from the target organizations identified in the tactical action plan.

—**Lead Qualification:** fast assessment of leads to determine their worth as an opportunity.

—**Systematic Pursuit:** the system for leading customers from lead opportunity to revenue earning sale.

—Most of your time in customer meetings should be spent listening, followed by asking pertinent questions.

—Every opportunity should be followed up with a proposal detailing the outcome for the customer should they use your offering.

—Following up every proposal for an update and feedback is essential to improving your win rate.

—Large or strategic opportunities should be tracked separately to maintain focus and effort.

—The business developer is the conduit of information between the market and your company. Make sure to develop a feedback loop to the leadership team to keep them current.

TRIPLE A: ACTION—FURTHER READING

—Donald Miller sets out a very simple sales process in his book *Business Made Simple: 60 Days to Master Leadership, Sales, Marketing, Execution, Management, Personal Productivity and More*. This puts it into context of the wider business.

—Once again, I recommend *Building a StoryBrand: Clarify Your Message So Customers Will Listen*, also by Donald Miller, to help frame your marketing messaging. This is very useful for LinkedIn posts and communications.

—Dixon and Adamson's book, *The Challenger Sale: Taking Control of the Customer Conversation*, displays an excellent customer conversation framework that leads the customer to understand why your offering is relevant and important.

—Stephen Covey's classic book *The 7 Habits of Highly Effective People* is gold. *Habit 5: First Seek to Understand* is essential when meeting customers for the first time.

Business Example: ACTION

With your plans all written, now is the time for action.

First, you look for a way to harness social media marketing to help keep the sales funnel full. During your discussions throughout the wider business, you realize that limited help is available from the central marketing team, who focuses on the larger engineering teams and the international project base. To get the message out and into the local sales ecosystem, you decide to set up your own marketing push on LinkedIn. You complete the following actions:

1. You change your profile, and that of your team, to really highlight the services of the WCS Consulting contaminated land team.

2. You commit to connect with thirty local contaminated land customers each day at multiple levels within the target organizations.

3. You dedicate time each week to write a brief post about a specific contaminated land issue, which educates the customer base and positions your team as experts in the field. These posts are only short, and you and the team already have ten written and ready to go.

The team members really get on board with this endeavor and collaborate on post writing and connecting with customers. You even get the service line leader in the USA involved by cross posting and engaging with their content.

Within a few weeks, the team's posts are generating interest, and customers are commenting about the content during face-to-face meetings.

Systematic Implementation

Following the process laid out in this book, you begin systematic implementation, and write down the qualification processes in line with WCS systems. Your qualification checklist questions are:

- ☐ Is this a business-as-usual request?
- ☐ Is the lead above our regular deal value of $30,000? If yes, involve the general manager (GM).
- ☐ Does the lead play to the strengths of our offering?
- ☐ Does the lead play to strengths of another department? If yes, involve the relevant team leaders.
- ☐ Will we require additional resources to win this lead? If yes, involve the GM.
- ☐ Is this an existing customer?
- ☐ Is the customer a good fit? If no, decline the opportunity.
- ☐ Does the lead come with an added level of risk? If yes, involve the GM.

You also write down the systematic pursuit process to remind yourself and the team where they are with each customer, and you add a couple of additional notes.

1. **Clarify**—what does the customer really want, and are there opportunities here for other WCS teams?
2. **Call**—remember to ask questions and listen.
3. **Meet**—is this a one-on-one meeting, or is there another specialist I should bring with me?
4. **Proposal**—follow the standard WCS proposal guidelines, but add the top three selling points in the introduction.
5. **Follow-Up Call**
6. **Adjust**
7. **Feedback Request**

Must-Win Opportunity Matrix

Large multidisciplinary projects are identified during the *aim* stage as a differentiator and valuable revenue stream for your team, and you know it is important to visually track these. You place a whiteboard on the office wall, and you draw a rough must-win opportunity matrix on it (figure 28).

Realizing the value of the cross-team collaboration, you develop a color-coded system with a different color for each lead discipline—green for environment, orange for infrastructure, and blue for the water division. This allows you to make sure that collaboration on the larger must-win projects is always front and center.

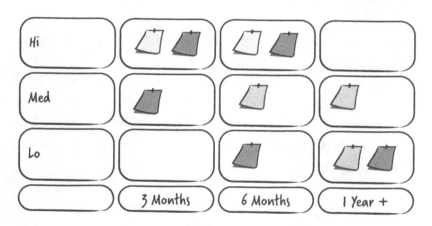

Figure 28: WCS Must-Win Opportunity Matrix

Each entry on the matrix has the following information included:

- **Project Name**
- **Type of Works**
- **Lead Company, or Company of Interest**
- **Key Contacts**
- **Timeframe**
- **Location**

The team decides to get together once a fortnight to discuss the board for thirty minutes—moving, adding, and removing opportunities as required. This results in the strategic opportunities being prioritized and proactive actions instigated, vastly improving the chance of a win.

Adaptive Feedback Loop

Finally, you realize you need a way to feedback the industry and market information that you and your team are gathering. In a moment of inspiration, it's clear that the meetings with internal stakeholders are the perfect mechanism, as they are already in place. To capitalize on this, you set yourself a goal to have at least one piece of market feedback information to share at each meeting, ensuring that it is properly disseminated to those who need to know. When urgent feedback is uncovered, you pass it on through a phone call or quick face-to-face discussion, which allows for a fast reaction if required.

Letting out a big breath, you smile. Your WCS team are ready to systematically enter the marketplace and begin their journey toward achieving significant business growth.

WCS ACTION Summary

I hope this example with WCS Consulting shows you that the *triple A framework* is a simple system to implement. While there is a bit of work upfront to get everything assessed and aligned, you can comfortably get yourself into the systematic implementation stage within a couple of weeks.

In this example, you had the luxury of involving your team in the planning and implementation—a good reminder to use the resources if you have them. Remember to use the *triple A* tools as a guide, altering them when necessary and ignoring the parts that don't fit your circumstances.

CONCLUSION

T hat wraps up your introduction to business development and the *triple A framework*. I hope you can see the value in having a simple system that keeps you focused on the important actions. The framework purposefully keeps away from hyper-detailed analysis, to make the process as simple and practical to implement as possible. It is designed to help guide your business development journey, not create lots of additional work.

Whether you are a consultant with business development as a section of your role, an entrepreneur with limited staff, or fully responsible for the business development function of your division, I hope you find parts of the framework that work for you and your team. Each reader's circumstances are different, so the framework is not a rigid set of rules. Use it to develop the tools that work for you and adjust them as you go.

This is just the tip of the iceberg. Keep on learning. Read and watch as much as you can around the topics of business development and sales. Become an expert in the field. Cherry-pick the parts that work for you and build upon the framework set out in this book.

Ultimately, your success comes down to your willingness to put in the work. Do the planning, organize the meetings, make the follow up, and keep that feedback flowing into your organization. Remember—without your action, there will be no results.

Finally, I truly hope the *triple A framework* brings you revenue growth and helps shape your business development journey as much as it shaped mine.

Good luck out there!

ACKNOWLEDGMENTS

Writing a book is a long process that would have been impossible without the support of my wife, Emma, who is always accepting of my many harebrained schemes and my 5 AM Saturday alarms. Also, for concocting the title, which is far superior to my previous efforts. Thank you for everything!

Mum and Dad inspired me to make the most out of life, and this book is evidence of that. I will always be grateful to you both for your belief in me, your support, and encouragement.

I know what it's like to be given business development responsibility with no guidance and absolutely no training. It can be confusing and overwhelming, and your efforts can easily be focused on the wrong direction. Luckily for me, I've had a series of strong mentors who helped me think about business systematically and logically. It is these lessons that have cemented my thinking, allowing me to shape the *triple A framework* into what it is today. Thanks to Andrew, Craig, Gordon, Greg, Jim, Shirley Anne, Steffi, and Wayne—I have truly appreciated your mentorship over the years and found your guidance invaluable.

Writing a manuscript is one thing, but shaping it into something readable is a crucial skill. For this, I must thank my editors Tracy

Everson and Miranda Dillon for their skilled suggestions in consistency and clarity. Also, Shirley Ann and Simon for reading my first draft and providing frank and invaluable feedback on flow and readability.

Thanks to Keith Turner for designing a series of coherent and stylish illustrations in a very short time frame indeed.

Getting a book into the hands of the reader takes more than just the author. There is a whole team of hardworking individuals behind the scenes. I'd like to thank John Koehler and the team at Koehler Books for their diligent efforts in getting this work out into the world.

REFERENCES

Chouinard, Yvon. *Let My People Go Surfing: The Education of a Reluctant Businessman*, New York: Penguin, 2005.

Collins, Jim, and Hansen, Morten T. *Great by Choice: Uncertainty, Chaos, and Luck—Why Some Thrive Despite Them All*. New York: Random House Books, 2011.

Covey, Stephen. *The 7 Habits of Highly Effective People*, New York: Free Press, 1989.

Dixon, Matthew, and Adamson, Brent. *The Challenger Sale: Taking Control of the Customer Conversation*, 1st ed. London: Penguin, 2011.

"Enduring Ideas: The GE-McKinsey nine-box matrix." *McKinsey Quarterly*, (September 2008).

Godin, Seth. *Purple Cow: Transform Your Business by Being Remarkable*. New York: Portfolio, 2003.

Hardwich G (2019-2020) Pers comms.

Kaplan, Robert S., and Norton, David P. "Mastering the Management System." *Harvard Business Review* 86, (January 2008): 62–77.

Kim, W. Chan, and Mauborgne, Renée. *Blue Ocean Strategy: How to Create Uncontested Market Space and Make the Competition Irrelevant*. Boston: Harvard Business School Press, 2005.

Levitt, Theodore. "Exploit the product life cycle." *Harvard Business Review*, vol 43, (November 1965): 81–94.

Lewis, RD. *When Cultures Collide: Managing Successfully Across Cultures*. London: Brealey Pub, revised 2006.

Miller, Donald. *Building a StoryBrand: Clarify Your Message So Customers Will Listen*. New York: Harper Collins, 2017.

Miller, Donald. (3 August 2020) "Tiffani Bova—How to Achieve (Smart) Growth for Your Company." Business Made Simple with Donald Miller, August 3, 2020.

Miller, Donald. *Business Made Simple: 60 Days to Master Leadership, Sales, Marketing, Execution, Management, Personal Productivity and More*, New York: Harper Collins, 2021.

Milligan, Jonathan. *Your Message Matters: How to Rise Above the Noise and Get Paid for What You Know*, Michigan: Baker Books, 2020.

Moore, Geoffrey A. *Crossing the Chasm: Marketing and Selling Disruptive Products to Mainstream Customers*, New York: HarperBusiness Essentials, 1991.

Pink, Daniel H. *To Sell Is Human: The Surprising Truth About Moving Others*, New York: Riverhead Books, 2012.

Porter, Michael. *Competitive Advantage*, New York: Free Press, 2004.

Sinek, Simon. *Start with Why*, New York: Penguin Books, 2011.

"The Lewis Model – Dimensions of Behaviour | Cross Culture." Crossculture.com. July 24, 2019. https://www.crossculture.com/the-lewis-model-dimensions-of-behaviour/.

Vance, Ashlee. *Elon Musk: How the Billionaire CEO of SpaceX and Tesla is Shaping our Future*, London: Virgin Books, 2016.

"What Is the Ansoff Matrix?" - A Guide to the Ansoff Product Market Growth Matrix. Accessed April 29, 2021. https://www.ansoffmatrix.com/.

Willink, Jocko, and Babin, Leif. *Extreme Ownership: How U.S. Navy SEALs Lead and Win.* Second edition. New York: St. Martin's Press, 2017.

Willink, Jocko. *The Dichotomy of Leadership with Leif Babin. Self-control, and how to find the balance* (episode 138). "Jocko Podcast," August 15, 2018.

ABOUT THE AUTHOR

Tom Watkin is an author and business leader with experience that spans the globe. He has led teams and business development efforts for organizations of all sizes over a range of industries. These have included startups, companies with limited market exposure, and those with strong existing customer bases.

This applied experience, coupled with an MBA, MSc, and BSc ensures that Tom can successfully bridge the communications gap between the technical, commercial, and sales disciplines. It has also allowed him to understand the hands-on and systematic application of strategy to business development to achieve repeatable results.

Tom lives in Fremantle, Western Australia, with his wonderful wife, two mischievous kids, and lazy cat. He loves family time, travel, outdoor adventures, and playing Dungeons & Dragons with his mates.

To find out more about the work Tom does, visit his website www.tomwatkin.com.

CPSIA information can be obtained
at www.ICGtesting.com
Printed in the USA
BVHW032242230623
666304BV00006B/810